David —

Found this in Santa Cruz
& thought of you

Much love

Judith

Zen in the Art of the
Tea Ceremony

Zen in the Art of the Tea Ceremony

HORST HAMMITZSCH

ST. MARTIN'S PRESS
NEW YORK

For information write:
St. Martin's Press Inc.,
175 Fifth Avenue, New York, N.Y. 10010

Library of Congress Catalog Card Number 80-53856

ISBN 0-312-89859-2

First published in the United States of America in 1981

Printed in Great Britain

Contents

Foreword

The concept 'Way' stands at the very heart of the cultural and intellectual life of Japan. It is the guiding principle of all the multifarious arts of the Japanese islands, and not least of the practice of ceremonial tea drinking. The Way is the tradition of any given art. In the absence of a Way there can be no progress for the practitioner of that art.

The Ways of Japan are many. And one of them is the Tea Way, *chadō* or *sadō*, to which we shall be devoting our attention here. Even in early times education and upbringing demanded that one should take up some Way, practise it, become a Man of that Way, *michi no hito*. If the Way was originally no more than an artistic technique to be acquired through zealous practice under a Master, this state of affairs started to change during medieval times and an important development resulted. The Way now started to become not only the repository of given skills but also of general principles, truths and teachings that could benefit the non-specialist, the layman. The Way became an educational tool for people generally. Since the Way represents a tradition, runs through many generations and will be passed on to further generations yet unborn, it embodies a sum of experiences that have arisen out of actual practice and are consequently of enduring importance for the Way in question. Tradition, in the Japanese sense, is not the passing on of something settled and finished that some Master has created. Far rather is it the transmission and continued 'living out' of a Master's whole being. Not only are the already mature aspects of a tradition passed on, but still immature, still growing elements are also included within it. It is precisely this that is important for the further development of the Way in question, for it is an essential aspect of that Way's wholeness, to which a learner or pupil can attain only when he masters the steps which lead to it.

This insight has a significant role to play in the mastering of the various arts, *gei*. For the term 'arts' should here be understood in the Far Eastern sense; the arts cover everything that is of value for the development of a person's character, for bringing the inner self nearer to perfection, for developing craft skills and intellectual skills alike, and thus in helping the person to attain full maturity.

In the pursuit of any given Way, the learner has to start by holding strictly to tradition – in other words, to the experience of that Way as transmitted and refined from generation to generation, and as represented in the form of concrete models, of oral tradition, or indeed of written transmission. He is permitted no freedom. The personal freedom of spontaneous activity is actually denied, as being not the true freedom that is to be striven for. Only when the learner has conquered his own wilfulness and schooled himself – re-experienced the received tradition in its entirety – can he recognize what is of eternal worth for the Way in question. Only then, having attained maturity, can he go on to such personal creations as now arise spontaneously from within him.

The most varied influences have contributed to the rise of such 'Way-consciousness' in Japan – among them, and to a quite remarkable extent, the powerful impulses that have emanated from Zen. It was, above all, the Zen teachings that left their spiritual stamp both on the outer forms and on the inner realities of the various Ways. We may regard as decisive the influence of the spirit of Zen on the Ways that started their actual development during the Kamakura period – and without a doubt the Tea Way is one of these. An expression such as *chazen-ichimi* (Tea Way and Zen are one) indicates clearly enough the close surviving connection. Almost all the Masters of the Tea Way had close links with Zen. It was its influence that first turned the tea cult into a genuine Tea Way. Strict self-discipline and the passing on of experience from mind to mind, *ishin-denshin*, are alone capable of being of real help to the individual on his Way.

Each of the Japanese Ways strives to penetrate the nature of the eternal, to experience All-Oneness. But this only succeeds when the seeker on the Way gives up the self and experiences selflessness, *muga*, and emptiness, *kū*. It is a silence so deep as to be audible, a sound which suddenly permits the listener to experience All-Oneness, once he has attained full maturity. And such a silence also reigns over the Tea Way, which in the last analysis represents the Way to the Self. He who has attained maturity along this Way, and who, by dint of the strictest self-discipline, has reached the goal of perfection in his craft, experiences in the small, empty tea-room that true freedom which transcends his tiny personal will. He experiences the freedom of the person who has liberated himself from all things that are bound up, even in the slightest degree, with the existent ego.

And if in present-day Japan the Tea Way still occupies an influential place, then the reason is surely to be found in the fact that, in Japan too, modern man is living in an age which in so many spheres of life has lost its centre, yet whose inhabitants still bear within themselves a longing for tranquillity. It is to this that the Tea Way shows them a path worth treading, even if a narrow one and difficult to follow. It leads man to the discovery of himself. The Grand Master Rikyū once declared: 'The art of the Tea Way consists simply of boiling water, preparing tea and drinking it.' How easy, how simple that sounds! And yet there are but few people who discover how to 'live' life, to be no longer dominated by the world 'out there', to surrender themselves wholly to whatever they are doing, to absorb themselves in it without thought and without fear of outer, irrelevant circumstances. To grasp the idea that 'One is in All and All in One', that the All cannot be separated from the One – that is the ultimate experience of this Way.

But it is a whole art to be 'perfectly imperfect' or, to use the words of an old Zen Master, not to gaze at the pointing finger when you would admire the full moon.

HORST HAMMITZSCH

By Way of Introduction

It was in about the third year of my time in Japan that I first came into contact with the Tea Way, the Tea Teaching, *chadō*. I had received an invitation to a *chakai*, a tea gathering, in Nagoya, at the home of a well-known Tea Master. So far I had not looked into the practice of this ceremonial form of tea drinking, and so I could approach this first experience of it quite objectively. In my diary I find the following notes:

A marvellous autumn day, the sky high and clear, illuminating in their deep red the leaves of the dwarf maples. The yellow foliage of the gingko trees, which enclose the garden against a range of hills, still radiates back the warmth of the dying day. Leaving the house forecourt, which is enclosed by a whitewashed wall capped with blue-grey tiles, I follow a path laid with large, round, dark-hued pebbles. Then I step through a gate made of bamboo wickerwork into the garden. Here I come to a halt. Is this garden really a world made by human hands? It is an entrancing landscape such as one finds in the coastal valleys of the Japanese islands, a landscape that reflects all the characteristics of those valleys. The visitor fancies that he can detect in the distance the roar of the sea, hear the playing of the sea breeze in the branches of ancient pines.

I follow the path, and it leads me to a simple hut with a shingle roof, nestling close against a grove of bamboos. Dark green moss spills from between its shingles. The place exudes an aura of secluded homeliness. I am the first guest to arrive at this *machiai*, or waiting-lodge. Here I shall meet the other guests invited by my friend the Tea Master, in order to go on and experience the Tea Ceremony, *chanoyu*, together.

The waiting-lodge is open towards the garden. It contains a simple bamboo bench. On this lie a few cushions of woven straw, and next to it stands an incense-burner. I sit down and look out across the garden. Here and there are groups of stones with moss and dwarf bamboo growing luxuriantly between them. The star-shaped blooms of clumps of wild asters twinkle white, lilac and dark red among the tree trunks. The crystal-clear water of a tiny stream hurries gaily over coloured pebbles, a symbol of the impermanence of all earthly existence. The panicles of the pampas-grass bow to the gentle autumn wind. The foliage of the bushes has already been thinned by this year's fall, and behind it there is a glimpse of woodwork of artful simplicity, betraying the presence of a small bridge. A picture of quiet solitude, of secluded tranquillity – such is this garden.

Soon the other guests appear. They are four in all. An aged scholar of distinguished bearing, a well-known painter and his wife, and a merchant who has his fine taste to thank for his reputation as an art collector. We greet each other, bowing deeply from the waist. Few comments are exchanged. Merely the odd word of praise for the layout of the garden, for the beauty of the autumnal colours, for our host's exquisite taste. For the most part, however, we devote ourselves to the silent enjoyment of this hour of inner self-recollection, its solemnity deepened even further by the gentle rustling of the bamboo leaves in the breeze.

Today the hospitable house of my friend, in which I have already passed so many entertaining and happy hours, has an unusual feel about it. The great entrance-doors were not open to greet me. The thronging servants were not standing ready, as they usually were, to welcome visitors. Only the old janitor in his darkly solemn kimono was there to receive me, and with hardly a word of greeting he led me to the little side-gate that leads to the path to the waiting-lodge. There he took his leave with a silent bow and withdrew.

And so the guest is left alone and without a guide to follow the narrow path that leads through the beauty of the garden to the silent, secluded waiting-lodge. And with every step into the depths of the garden, the everyday world, with its bustling haste, fades from the mind. One steps into a world that is free of everyday pressures, forgets the whys and ceases to enquire into the wherefores. The deeper the guest penetrates into the garden, this world of solemn tranquillity, the freer he becomes of everyday cares. The other guests, too, seem to have become changed people. The scholar, normally so reserved, is more communicative; the painter has lost his strong tendency to engage in aesthetic argument, the merchant his preoccupation with business deals. All of them have forgotten the everyday things that normally rule their lives from early morning until late at night. Casting them off, they have committed themselves unreservedly to this world of silence, of inner freedom.

After a short wait our host appears on the path that leads out of the grove of bamboos. With a serious, solemn air he strides towards us. At a certain distance from us, he stops, bows low. That is his greeting. No word, no other gesture. Then he turns around and walks back along the path. Now he is ready to receive his guests – that is the meaning of this little ritual.

A moment of stillness follows. Then the *shōkyaku*, the principal guest, bows to the other guests and follows the host. In no particular order and at short intervals the others follow suit. I am the third guest to leave the waiting-lodge.

The path first leads for a short distance through the bamboo grove. Here the cicadas are shrilling their last song. Then the path slopes gently downhill. Clumps of sweet clover are displaying their pale pink blooms to right and left of the path. But this is no garden path in the European sense. The visitor is guided by a series of single stones, each set at a distance of a pace from its predecessor. *Tobiishi*, stepping-stones, they are called. Between the stones, rich green moss and thick shiba-grass luxuriate. Other paths cross our own. Occasional smaller stones, laid on the stepping-stones, show the walker which direction is closed to him. These small stones, called *tomeishi*, are inviolable barriers. Slowly I follow the windings of the path, hesitating here and there to admire the skilfully-contrived 'natural' views of the garden landscape. There is no longer the slightest hint of their man-made nature. Via a bridge I cross the stream and then find myself standing before a large, flat stone. A basin has been hewn out of its surface, and fresh spring-water trickles softly into it out of a bamboo pipe. A simple bamboo scoop lies beside the basin. A short distance away there rises a stone lantern, grey with age, its gently curving roof festooned with plaited hangings.

I take up the scoop, dip it into the water of the basin, fill it and take a sip of its contents to rinse out my mouth. The rest I let run over my hands. In this way I perform a symbolic purification. Now even the last dust clinging to me from that earthly world has been washed away. Clean and free, I can enter the world of tea and stillness.

Only a few more steps and there – I am brought to a sudden halt – what a symphony of art and nature, what an ensemble of perfect imperfection! There it is, the *chashitsu*, the tea-room. Expression of an indescribable taste; artistic and yet not artificial, consciously conceived and yet so pure in form and so natural in construction that it seems almost unbelievable to behold. Can the human creative spirit have produced such a work of nature? One might call the tea-room a mere hut, but for the fact that it displays this extraordinary refinement of taste. A deeply overhanging thatched roof, thick with moss. The guttering a length of split bamboo. The walls clad half in reed-wattles, half in daub. The entrance a low sliding-door covered with rice-paper of spotless white. In front of it, the stone threshold.

Bending low, I slip into the tea-room, walk slowly to the alcove – *tokonoma* – which lies diagonally opposite the door, sink to my knees before it and bow deeply to the floor. Then I contemplate the flower-arrangement that stands in the alcove. In a bamboo vase stands a branch bearing red berries against a background of autumnal foliage to which, like drops of dew, pearls of water are clinging. Next, after another slight bow, I stand up and take my place beside the guest who preceded me. The guests sit with their backs to the rice-papered sliding-doors that shut off the tea-room from the garden.

Not until the guests have all assembled does the host appear. Consequently I have time to examine the room. Four and a half *tatami* – mats of rice-straw with a covering of rushes – cover the floor and at the same time establish the size of the tea-room as being some nine square metres in area. The flowers in the *tokonoma* provide the only decoration. In the centre of the room a piece of *tatami* has been left out. The space is occupied by the fire-pit with its dark wooden edging. Within it, a cone of fine ash has been brushed together to half-conceal the glowing charcoal. A heavy iron kettle stands on a tripod over the fire, its colour bespeaking great antiquity. On a small stand I see an incense-burner and a small feather-duster. Otherwise the room is without adornment. Unless, that is, one classes as ¤pornment the exquisite graining of the woodwork that divides up the dark wall-surfaces, or the timber-clad ceiling.

As soon as we guests have begun to converse softly – a sign that we have concluded our contemplation of the tea-room – the host enters. He does so through a sliding-door that screens off the *mizuya*, the room which is used for preparing the Tea Ceremony. Kneeling down, he bows deeply to his guests. Then he disappears through the door again, returning at once with various utensils – a basket of charcoal, lifting-rings for raising the kettle from the fire, and so on. He also brings in a pan of fine ash. Then he settles down at the fire-pit, takes off the kettle, makes up the fire and heaps more ashes on top of the charcoal. He also sprinkles incense on the fire. During these manoeuvres we have all moved closer to the fire and have been watching attentively. Now, however, we resume our original places. The chief guest asks the Tea Master if he may examine the incense-holder more closely. The Tea Master duly brings the holder to where the guest is sitting and sets it thoughtfully down on his *fukusa*, a small piece of silken cloth. This cloth has an important role to play in supporting the tea utensils while they are being examined. The chief guest unfolds his own *fukusa*, a rich lilac in colour, and transfers the vessel onto his own cloth. Then he examines it thorough-ly, and finally it is passed from guest to guest, until the last one hands it back gratefully to the host. The latter goes back into the *mizuya*, only to return and announce that the 'simple meal' will now be served. One at a time he brings in five trays, one for each guest. The number of courses is less than at the usual Japanese ceremonial meal, but for that reason the dishes are of choicer quality and most tastefully prepared. Even the cutlery displays exquisite taste. With a slight bow we receive the trays and take them with both hands from the host. The drink is hot *sake*, rice-wine. Finally, sweets are handed around. And so the tea meal, *kaiseki*, comes to an end. With a bow the host invites his guests to rest a little, and withdraws. Bowing once more before the *tokonoma*, we leave the tea-room in the same order as we entered it and make our way back to the waiting-lodge.

In the waiting-lodge a conversation strikes up, and the odd guest even lights up a cigarette or a little Japanese pipe. However, after a short interval, the sound of a gong reverberates from the tea-room – long, penetrating gong-beats, five in number. Our conversation ceases on the first beat, and gives way to a reverent silence. One feels as though transported to a Zen temple in some secluded mountain-cleft. The atmosphere is solemn.

Once again the chief guest is the first to take the path back to the tea-room. We others follow in the same order as before. Between the stones and on the path itself stand small bamboo lanterns, for dusk is now falling. At the water-basin each once again performs the purification ceremony and then re-enters the tea-room.

There, the flowers in the alcove have now given way to a hanging scroll. It bears a simple black-and-white drawing representing a broom made of bamboo shoots. On the fire in the fire-pit, the water in the kettle is gently singing. On the *tatami* a *mizusashi* (a water jar) and the *cha'ire* (the tea-caddy) are standing in their prescribed places. As soon as all the guests are present, the Tea Master appears. He is carrying the tea-bowl with both hands. In the tea-bowl lies the *chasen*, the tea-whisk (a brush made of bamboo) and the *chakin*, a narrow, white linen cloth. Across the tea-bowl lies the tea-scoop, *chashaku*. Going out again, he then brings back a water-vessel for used water, *koboshi*, the water-dipper, *hishaku*, and the lid-stand, *futa'oki*, for the hot lid of the kettle. The tea-whisk, the white linen cloth and the water-dipper are new and sparkling clean. The rest of the tea utensils are clearly of great age and bear witness to a highly-developed artistic taste.

The Master sits down in the prescribed attitude, and the actual ceremony now begins. In a precisely predetermined series of gestures and movements, each individual part of the ceremony is performed in its correct sequence. The folding of the teacloth, the grasping of the water-dipper, the rinsing out of the tea-bowl with hot water, the opening of the tea-caddy, the dusting of the tea-scoop, the movements of tea-whisking – all this is firmly established by tradition and is carried out strictly according to the rules of the school in question.

While the host is attending to the initial preparations, the first guest takes one of the proferred sweet cakes and hands on the cake-stand to the next guest in the manner laid down. Then the host places the bowl of thick, green, whisked tea in front of the first guest. Mutual bows ensue, as well as a further bow on the part of the first guest to the one sitting next to him, as though to beg forgiveness for drinking before him. Only then does he take the tea-bowl, placing it on the palm of his left hand and supporting it with his right. He takes one sip, then a second and a third, each time gently swilling the bowl around. With a thin piece of white paper he then wipes clean the place on the rim from which he has drunk, and passes on the bowl to the next guest, the prescribed bows once more being duly exchanged. And so on, in turn.

One praises the taste of the tea, its strength, its colour, and generally speaks of such things as will fill the host with pleasure. All conversation in the tea-room takes place on a level far from everyday things. One speaks of painters, poets, Tea Masters and their achievements, of the tastes and opinions of various periods, of the exquisite tea utensils.

When the ceremony is at an end, the first guest asks if he may examine the utensils. And now there commences a detailed examination of the tea-bowl, the tea-caddy and the teaspoon. Questions and answers are exchanged between guests and host. We enquire about the origin and history of the tea utensils, the names of the craftsmen who made them, for every good piece has its own individual history.

The tea-bowl in use today is a simple, ivory-coloured bowl with a glaze of a dull green hue. Not until I hear that it has been in the family for two hundred years, that an ancestor received it as a gift from his feudal lord for some memorable deed, do I grasp its true value. As for the value of the tea-scoop – a simple, narrow, bamboo spoon – this remains unknown to me.

What impression did I take away with me from this first Tea Ceremony? It engendered in me a special feeling that reminded me of an experience I had had in my homeland some years before. We were hiking in southern Germany, and visiting one of those especially delightful village-churches. With us was a friend, a musician by calling and profession. He sat down at the organ and began to play Bach. And suddenly, with the music filling the whole body of the church, I felt that space ceased to exist and only the flood of notes still remained. I, too, seemed as though divested of all materiality, totally absorbed in the music. And here in Japan I had now had a similar experience. The effect of the Tea Ceremony was so strong as to engender a feeling of self-surrender, a feeling of oneness with all others, an extraordinary feeling of satisfaction with myself and with my surroundings . . .

So much, then, for my diary-notes. My first encounter with this form of tea drinking had impressed me deeply, and encouraged me to look into it further. It was not so much the outer form of the ceremony that interested me as its hidden inner meaning. Here my experience as a specialist in Japanese culture was to come in useful. As part of my researches I could now delve into the numerous works that dealt with tea, with the ceremonial way of drinking it, with the nature of the special tea doctrine, the Tea Way. What is more, I had many Japanese friends who were followers of the Tea Way – followers not merely in the sense of mastery of its forms, but in a much deeper sense. They were truly in search of the ultimate, the most profound. For them the Tea Ceremony was no mere aesthetic amusement, not just a training in etiquette. They were *chajin*, tea-people, to the very core.

From my diary-notes, however, even though these give a picture only of the outer form of that ceremony, one fact will nevertheless already be apparent. There are innumerable rules to master before one can proceed to the performance of such a ceremony. The rules are interlinked so closely, and in so organised a manner, that each always proceeds – must proceed – quite inevitably from the one before it. In fact the rules in their totality are so numerous, so comprehensive, that at first sight they seem to leave no room for the addition of any personal touch to either tea cult or Tea Ceremony. And yet such is not the case. Many Tea Masters actually emphasize the personal, creative aspect. We shall be seeing later how creativity can transcend the rules and yet fit in with their various categories. Of this there are numerous examples.

The most basic principle underlying these rules is that everything must be in harmony with its surroundings; it must be simple, yet eschew the actual natural state itself; it must be honest – thus its true nature and construction must be recognizable and devoid of all pretence. And just as everything must be in harmony with its surroundings, so it must also stand in a harmonious relationship with the wider environment – with the seasons, for example. Winter imposes different constraints from summer on fireplace, temperature and similarly on the form of utensils. All these fine gradations and distinctions are extremely well-founded. Even the attitudes and movements of host and guests are subject to rules whose detailed rubric cannot be gone into here. The real question we shall be trying to answer is, where does the Tea Way lead? What is the ultimate goal of the tea teaching? In answering it we can hardly avoid considering a number of matters pertaining to formal art, but we shall do so only when they have a decisive bearing on questions of inner attitude.

A true understanding of the Tea Way can be achieved only from the roots up – through the story of its origins and development. Although the custom of tea drinking, even in its ceremonial form, has been known in Japan since early times, what we know today as the Tea Way is more than just a particular way of drinking. It embodies an attitude that is quite unique. The nature of this attitude can be truly grasped only when one is aware of all the influences that have given rise to it, caused it to grow and, in the course of a long process of maturation, modified it. We shall not be able here to indicate every single event along that path, for so much of it has been, to quote the words of one Tea Master, 'ephemeral as the morning dew on the stalks of the rice-plants'.

A Japanese will speak of *chadō*, of the Tea Way. There are many such Ways in Japan. There is a Way of Flowers, a Way of Painting, a Way of Poetry and numerous others. Each of the Japanese arts possesses its own Way. What inner significance, then, does the concept 'Way' (Jap., *michi*, Sinojap., *dō*, Chin., *tao*) hold? This is the question that first demands our attention.

A Way comes from somewhere and leads to somewhere. Its goal is the grasping of eternal values, of Truth, *makoto*. In the process it acts as a strict guardian of tradition – which carries a valuation very different to that in Europe. Thus, in the Japanese view, it maintains an unbroken link between past, present and future. On this foundation is based the Master-pupil relationship that is so important for the development of the Japanese arts. It is seen as vital that the pupil should start by achieving a sure mastery of traditional ways.

In Japan, the learning of any one of the many arts is an almost wordless process. The Master supplies the model, the pupil copies it. This process is repeated again and again, month after month, year after year. For the Japanese learner this constitutes far less of a test of patience than it might seem to us. From childhood on, his method of upbringing has prepared him for it. The Master seeks nothing in the pupil, no gift, no genius. He simply trains the pupil fully to master the pure skills of the art in question. Once this mastery is attained, a day will eventually come when the pupil is able to represent perfectly what is there in his heart*, precisely because the problem of formulation, of mere technical realization, no longer burdens him. Only when the heart has attained maturity does true spontaneity arise. Even art must, like every natural being, grow organically: it can never create by act of will.

An example may illustrate this teaching technique. A young German girl was studying Japanese painting in Japan under the Master Morimura Gitō. As she had already taken up sculpture some time before, the purely technical side came easily to her. The Master, for his part, recognized the fact, though without deviating at all from his Way. Whenever she came for her lesson, he arranged his brushes, rubbed ink on the rubbing-stone, set out the colours and painted her a picture, a design, which she then had to copy until the next lesson. In this way month gave way to month, year to year. After two years the pupil finally lost patience. One day she surprised the Master with a picture of her own devising. He looked at

---

* I propose to retain here the Japanese sense of the word 'heart', *kokoro*, in its wider meaning of heart, soul, mind and spirit.

the painting for a long time, and even longer at his pupil. Then, without a word, he reached for his brush, dipped it in red ink and drew a thin line right across the piece of 'art'. The pupil was bitterly disappointed. How splendid her painted landscape's well-thought-out composition had seemed to her!

Months later the Master was sitting in his pupil's summer-house. While she prepared tea, he was looking critically through her sketches that were lying on the table. Suddenly he asked, 'Where did this one come from?' 'Oh, it's nothing, just a sketch, a doodle!' came the answer. For a long time the Master said nothing. Then he spoke, 'This is it, this is the Way!'

It is not conscious composition that makes a picture: far from it. The picture must come from within, from the heart. It is there as soon as the pupil has attained maturity; it comes spontaneously, without anybody's assistance.

Such are the workings of the Way. Only in this manner can it be trodden. Throughout the centuries-old development of Japanese culture, we find many voices constantly re-emphasizing the fact. Yoshida Kenkō (1283–1350), a courtier under various emperors and eventually a hermit-recluse and monk, writes in his *Tsurezuregusa* ('Notes in Leisure-Hours'):

> ... if a person follows the Way strictly and is not haphazard about it, he will finally, in the course of the years – and far sooner than one of exceedingly great talent who is not so well prepared – attain the ranks of eminence and, recognized by men for his achievements, make for himself a name without compare. Even among those who are now regarded by the world as eminent, there have been such as initially were reputed to be untalented and who committed extraordinary mistakes. Nevertheless, because they held strictly to the Way's demands, deemed it important and concentrated wholly

on it, they became models in this world and teachers for all. This applies equally to all Ways.

The experience of craftsmanship accumulated during the study of a Way eventually bestows its fruit on the learner who, after years of practice, attains one of the various goals. He becomes a true individual. It is only much later that he becomes a Master.

Only when a person is rid of all attachment to things, of all his ties with this earthly world, does his heart become free. The Tea Way, too, pursues this goal, and at its centre stands man himself. Tea Master and guests alike strive to attain perfection, just as a painter perfects his picture, a poet his verse.

Tea in Japan, its Origins and Use

Hundreds of years were to elapse before tea rose in Japan from its function as a mere medicinal drink and stimulant to become the focus of social gatherings, master in its own house among people of like mind. Not until it had burst out of the walls of monastery and temple, broken through the class barriers and forsaken the imperial court did it at last draw the entire Japanese people under its spell. Through the efforts of the great Tea Masters, tea and the manner of taking it attained their ultimate perfection. The tea teaching, the Tea Way, *chadō*, arose. Grand Masters such as Shukō, Jōō and Rikyū appeared, took over and reinforced the old, created the new and gave the teaching its inner meaning. Of the followers of the Tea Way they demanded not merely an artistic and craftsmanlike mastery of tea preparation and drinking; they required a particular attitude to life as such. The teaching became a criterion for living.

Among all the multifarious Ways of Japan, the Tea Way holds a special place, attracting more disciples than any other of the Japanese arts. Historically, it has been now pre-eminent, now apparently neglected and forgotten.

The history of tea in Japan displays a series of well-marked phases: after the new drink had become well-known in China, we have its first appearance and earliest use in Japan, the institution of tea competitions, the growth of the Tea Way, its first flowering, its neglect and decay, its resuscitation and perfection, and the subsequent refinement and consolidation of the tradition.

The home of tea drinking was China. Tea was already known there in early times, as ancient sources reveal. Initially it was used as a medicament and later, it seems, as a drink, but the manner of preparing and drinking it was primitive. Its use became more widespread during the era of the Six Dynasties (420–588), and its status as a drink more firmly established. It was only in the T'ang period (618–906), however, that tea was to become a highly-esteemed commodity. Lu Yü (d.804), a poet and aesthete, was the real pioneer of tea and the way of drinking it. He composed the 'tea-classic', *Ch'a-ching*. In this three-volume work the author deals with the tea plant, how to grow it, the harvesting of the tea-leaves, the utensils used for preparing tea, the preparation process itself and the various possible forms of ceremonial tea drinking. It is of interest to find already mentioned here utensils which were later to be used in identical form in the Japanese Tea Ceremony. To this work, probably written in around the year 772, we owe much valuable information on the development and form of tea drinking in China. It rapidly became known among Lu Yü's friends – monk-poets, painters and *literati* – who duly spread it far and wide. Tea became fashionable, as a drink whose consumption was governed by certain conventions. Here one can detect the first beginnings of the Tea Way in China.

In the T'ang era, tea was used in the form of *dancha* (Chin., *t'uan-ch'a*) or *dashicha* (Chin., *yen-ch'a*). The tea-leaves were steamed, pounded in a tea-mortar and moulded into a cake, pieces of which could then be cut off as needed. These were boiled up with other aromatic ingredients and the whole concoction was then drunk. In other words it was a kind of brick-tea, such as is still used today. The tea used by the Japanese monks during the Nara period (710–782) was of this type.

During the Sung period (960–1279) this boiled tea gave way to pulverized tea, *matcha* (Chin., *mo-ch'a*) or *hikicha* (Chin., *nien-ch'a*), which very rapidly replaced the tea of the T'ang period. The young shoots of specially-cultivated tea plants would be harvested at the proper time, put into a sack and subsequently stored in it, sealed inside a great stone jar. After some ten months the seal would be broken, the leaves pulverized in a tea-mortar and the dust poured into the tea-bowl, whisked and drunk. This type of tea became known and much-prized in Japan around the beginning of the Kamakura period (1222–1333). It is this pulverized tea that is still used today in the Tea Ceremony.

Meanwhile, if tea had changed its form during the Sung era, so, too, had the tea ideal. There were deep underlying reasons for this change, however. What was it that the T'ang era had bequeathed to the succeeding Sung period to fructify this new growth and development? Such is the point at which we need to start our investigation.

It was a variety of significant teachings, their similar values and overlapping views, that formed the basis for the development of the philosophical and intellectual climate of the new era. For a start, there was Confucianism, standing with both feet upon the earth of perceived reality. To it deferred the positive and practical aspect of the Chinese mentality. The emotional side of the Chinese, their *penchant* towards the mystical, was claimed by Taoism, which here opened up all kinds of possible further developments. Buddhism, which had come to China in very early times, was also at work, and its representatives were by now well aware of how to adapt the world of Indian thought, with its alien intellectual tradition, to the people's inner needs.

The change in intellectual attitudes was reflected in all spheres of life. And if formal tea drinking had been more or less symbolic during the T'ang era, one particular form of tea drinking now became a sacred act. It became, as Kakuzō Okakura puts it, a path to self-realization.* The

* Kakuzō Okakura, *The Book of Tea*, Dover Publications, New York, 1964.

devotees of the southern school of Zen helped to bring about this development, having themselves developed a Tea Ceremony whose performance followed strict ritual procedure. In front of the picture of China's first Zen patriarch, Bodhidharma (Chin., Ta-Mo), who arrived in China around 520 or 527, the monks drank tea communally out of a bowl. Only in Japan would this tradition be preserved, like so much of the cultural inheritance of the Sung period which fell into oblivion under the Mongol Yüan rule. This form of tea drinking became in Japan the prototype of the Tea Ceremony that we find later in the Ashikaga period (1336–1573).

The Sung dynasty had an unhappy time trying to preserve the stability of the state. And yet, despite military feuds, disorders and uprisings, almost all spheres of cultural activity flourished during this period. Numerous eminent scholars, philosophers, historians, poets and painters, priests and monks participated in this development, as well as many anonymous craftsmen and artists.

During the periods which followed, the refined form of tea drinking sank into oblivion, as also did the special types of tea appropriate to it. In the Ming era (1368–1661) the tea-leaves were steeped in hot water and the resulting tea consumed. This was tea in its *sencha* (Chin., *chien-ch'a*) or *hacha* (Chin., *yeh-ch'a*) form, which was popular in Japan during the Edo period. It was in this form that Europe first made the acquaintance of tea, for it was only in the year 1610 that the ships of the Dutch East India Company first brought tea to Europe.

It is not possible to discover any firm date for the introduction of tea to Japan. However, it was already in use during the Nara period, and there can be little doubt that there were Japanese monks and envoys during the T'ang period who got to know and prize it in the monasteries of China and at the Chinese court, subsequently bringing it back with them to Japan in the form of seeds or seedlings. There it established itself first of all in the Buddhist seminaries and schools. The first mention of the use of tea in the Japanese written records occurs in the year 729. After relations with China had been broken off in the year 895, and with the development of an independent Japanese culture, the practice and custom of tea drinking went into rapid decline, being preserved only in the monasteries and temples. The form of tea and its preparation during this period was that of the T'ang era.

It was the monk and Zen Master Eisai (1141–1215) who was to revive the custom of tea drinking once more. On two occasions Eisai had visited China under the Sung régime, and while there had studied the teachings of Zen and learnt from the Chinese monks the secrets of the use of pulverized tea. At the same time he had also made himself thoroughly familiar with the culture of the tea bush. After his return he laid out tea plantations in the grounds of the Ryōzen temple in the old province of Bizen on Kyūshū, and there planted out the seeds he had brought with him. Later he transplanted the young tea bushes to the Shōfoku temple at Hakata. As for the knowledge of tea that he had acquired in China from the local Zen monks, he set this all down in a two-volume work, *Kissayōjōki* (1211). In it he explains the benefits of tea drinking and acquaints the reader with the cultivation of the tea plant and the preparation of pulverized tea. When the last Shōgun of the house of Minamoto, Sanemoto (1204–1219), fell ill, Eisai sent him a bowl of tea, together with his work *Kissayōjōki*. The patient recovered, and Sanemoto, embarking on a study of the work, began to set great store by this form of tea drinking. It was in this way that the health-giving properties of tea first acquired their reputation, in which connection Eisai writes in his book, 'As a life-preserver, tea is a real healing-drink, a secret remedy for prolonging life.'

Meanwhile, Eisai had presented some tea seeds to his pupil Myōe (1173–1232), a famous monk of the Kegon school, who had studied Zen and his tea teachings with him. Myōe planted the seeds experimentally in the vicinity of his temple, which lay at Toganoo, in the north-west of Kyōto, the capital. Thanks to the good soil, a first-class crop resulted. In the tea competitions of later times, this tea was known as *honcha* or *moto no cha*, the 'original tea', in contradistinction to the varieties of tea produced by other tea-gardens, which were known as *hicha*.

And so it was Eisai and Myōe who did much to spread the custom of tea drinking, even if initially still within the context of monastic life. Tea helped to ward off sleepiness during meditation exercises and strengthened the monks' concentration. At the same time it was also held to be a first-rate medicine, as we have already seen. But it was still a means to an end.

It was the priest Eison of the Saidai temple at Nara who introduced tea to a wider public. In the year 1262 he was invited by Hōjō Sanetoki (1224–1275) to Kamakura. On the way there he regaled with tea the poor and the sick of the various provinces he passed through, as described in his travelling diary, *Kantō-ōenki*. He also observed the same custom in the Saidai temple at Nara. Here the tea which was left over from the tea-offering to the statue of the Buddha was afterwards offered to the monks and the faithful. This custom of dispensing tea was called *secha*. In time it became universally popular, and a variety of sources refer to the practice.

Thus it was that, through the influence of the Zen priests, the use of powdered tea came to be further cultivated in the temples and monasteries around the beginning of the Kamakura period. Via the teachings of Zen it then found its way into further circles. As well as the nobility and the warrior class, the common people too made its acquaintance, through its association with religious ceremonies. But what brought about its even more vigorous propagation was the introduction of the tea competitions that had already been universally popular in China during the Sung era. These tea competitions, *tōcha* (Chin., *tou-ch'a*) flourished especially in Japan during the period between the mid-fourteenth century and the end of the sixteenth. They satisfied the Japanese *penchant* for social gregariousness and fitted in admirably with the social competitions known by the name *monoawase*. Where previously these had revolved around poems, flowers, insects, herbs, shellfish and so on, now it was tea. The guests were offered a variety of teas, generally four, and had to decide which sort was *honcha* (tea produced at Toganoo and later at Uji) and which sorts were *hicha* (tea produced by other tea-gardens). We find reports of such tea competitions in a book entitled *Kissaōrai*, attributed to the monk Gen'e. The author recounts that such tea competitions took place in about the sixth month. The guests would first assemble on the ground-floor of a tea pavilion, where they were offered refreshments. After greeting them, the host or organiser would lead them to the tea-room on the floor above, where the tasting of the various teas was to take place. From this room, which was surrounded by a gallery, there were views to all four quarters of the compass. The Gold and Silver Pavilions, Kinkakuji and Ginkakuji, in Kyōto, are the best extant examples of such tea pavilions.

Once the guests had entered the tea-room, they would find a picture of the Buddha hanging on the main wall with, on either side of it, other pictures by famous artists illustrating the Buddha's teachings. Alternatively, this might be replaced by a picture of the holy Kwannon

(Avalokitesvara). From a table in front of it would be hanging a piece of gold brocade surmounted by a bronze Chinese flower-urn. Perfume-jars and tea-urns would all be in place. On ornamental trays on the west side of the room, rare fruits would be displayed, while on the north side the prizes for eventual distribution would be on show. Behind these stood the water-kettle, its water already on the boil. The guests would settle down on their seats, over which leopard-skins were stretched. The sliding-doors of the room were decorated with a variety of Chinese paintings.

Once the company had assembled, the host's son would offer fruit to the guests in strict order of precedence. After that, the tea would be handed out, and the actual competition would begin. The participants would gain points according to the accuracy of their judgement, and on this basis the appropriate prizes would be allotted. At the end of the tea tasting the tea utensils would be cleared away, and a joyous banquet of choice fish-dishes and rice-wine would commence.

Even though these tea competitions had as yet nothing to do with the Tea Way as such, they nevertheless prepared the ground for the new teaching. From the formal point of view they already contained much that later reappeared or was retained in the Tea Ceremony. The heavily Chinese-orientated canon of taste was to change, and things Japanese would take over the tea-room which itself developed out of the tea pavilion. The pictures of the Buddha, too, and the representations of Buddhist saints, would give way to pictures of landscapes, flowers and animals in the course of time. The tasting would fade more and more into the background, with the social reunion becoming the chief *raison d'être* of the occasion.

The latter tea gatherings were called *unkyaku-chakai*, and on such occasions low-grade tea was drunk and a communal bath taken. In the bathroom, small, decorated screens, flowers, vases and incense-holders were installed, and even in the tea-room itself two scrolls of calligraphy were hung up on the east and west walls, complemented by tastefully-arranged flowers and more screens. After the bath, tea was drunk, of which there were two types – one of them Uji tea. By way of fruit there were white melons and mountain peaches, accompanied by buckwheat-noodles. There is no trace here of the rich ostentation of the former tea competitions of the capital city. Pictorial decorations and flowers were chosen in accordance with personal taste, and rare tea utensils seem no longer to have been employed. It was a quite different spirit that ruled these gatherings.

The designation of a tea gathering as a *Chanoyu* was to become established even before the time of the great Tea Masters. If, however, one renders the term *chanoyu* as 'Tea Ceremony', this translation is justified only if certain fixed rules are observed, such as to give the occasion a ceremonial character. Naturally, the tea competitions also followed certain rules, but these were in no way immutable. On these occasions a host could follow his own taste – even though the general principles remained constant. It was only through the influence of the warrior class, whose whole lives were similarly ruled by a strict code of conduct, that the Tea Ceremony was to acquire its more rigid framework of rules. The first to turn their attention to the problems of codifying their class's etiquette were the warrior clan of the Ogasawara in the province of Shinano, who were to bring out the twelve-volume *Sangi-ittō-sōshi* at the behest of the Shōgun Ashikaga Yoshimitsu (1367–1395). It was Ogasawara Nagahide who finally completed the work, along with Imagawa Ujiyori and Ise Mitsutada, basing his efforts on the preparatory studies undertaken by his grandfather Ogasawara Sadamune, the formulation of which was strongly influenced by the work of the monk Dōgen and by his everyday rules for a strict and simple, Zen-based lifestyle. Such prescriptions for warriors' etiquette covered every aspect of life, and among them the rules for tea drinking had a by no means unimportant role to play. On the other hand it should be made clear that with time these rules were to deviate more and more from those used in the Zen monasteries, eventually acquiring distinct forms of their own.

A figure who left a particularly lasting impression on the formulation of the rules for tea gatherings, meanwhile, was a Master who enjoyed the unusual privilege of being adviser and director in matters of artistic taste at the house of the Shōguns. This Master was Nōami (1397–1471). Not only did he enjoy a reputation as a contemporary Tea Master, but he also distinguished himself as a painter of ink-drawings, as a Master of linked-verse, *renga*, and as a Master of classical flower-arrangement. Brought in by the sixth Ashikaga Shōgun, Yoshinori (1428–1441), he soon became his confidant in all artistic matters. Nōami devoted himself intensively to questions relating to the use of tea utensils, which at this time gained new significance as a result of an architectural change. Where previously the tea gatherings of the *tōcha* had taken place in tea pavilions, for the most part two-storeyed, they were now transferred into the actual living-quarters of the warriors and nobles.

In the course of the Middle Ages a new house-layout had gradually developed out of the residential style favoured by the court nobility, the *shindenzukuri*. This development was due to the influence of the Zen priests, who enjoyed the closest of relationships with the developing warrior class. In the monasteries the priests' cells were fitted with an alcove, *tokonoma*, in which the Buddha's picture was placed. Next to it a niche was installed, with staggered shelves, *chigaidana*, to take the

Buddhist scriptures, as well as a kind of bay window, *shoin*, for reading or working. Adjoining the main room, a special anteroom, *genkan*, was added – such as may still be found to this day in Japanese-style dwellings. With the new building style, then, the reading bay of the Zen monks found its way into contemporary domestic architecture, which ever since has borne the stylistic label *shoinzukuri*.

It was into this main room with its *shoin* that the tea gathering was now transferred. But this fact in turn had further, radical consequences for its outward form and procedure. Leaning heavily on the custom of the tea competitions, Nōami created the basis of a new style of tea gathering, which came to be known as *shoin no chayu*. The style and manner of arranging the various ornaments, pictures and tea utensils was referred to as *shoin-kasari*. Two or three thematically-interrelated picture-scrolls were hung up in the alcove. In front of these were placed the incense-burner, the flower vase and the candle-holder. Opposite the window of the reading bay stood a table equipped with rubbing-stone, ink, brush and water container. On the shelves were displayed incense-burners of various kinds and other items of taste and value. The *shoin-kasari* was designed to bring a spiritual dimension of solemn beauty into the tea-room.

Of special importance for the further development of the Tea Ceremony, however, was the use of the stand known as *daisu*, which pertained to the supplementary equipment used for the ceremony. This stand, which consisted of an upper and a lower shelf joined by either two or four supports, was designed to carry a special arrangement of tea utensils. On the lower shelf stood, on the left, the charcoal-brazier, *furo*, with the iron water-kettle, *kama* and, on the right, the jar for the cold water, *mizusashi*. Between them, a receptacle containing the water-dipper, *hishaku*, and the pair of iron rods, *hibashi*, for tending the fire. In front of this, the bowl for waste water, *mizukoboshi*. On the upper shelf were placed the tea-bowl, *chawan* – often containing the tea-whisk, *chasen*, the linen teacloth, *chakin*, and the bamboo tea-scoop, *chashaku* – and the tea-caddy, *cha'ire*.

In addition, Nōami instituted rules for etiquette in the tea-room itself, as well as laying down the correct procedure for bringing in and manipulating the utensils Here he no longer based his prescriptions specifically on the rules of the tea competitions, but on the code of etiquette of the warrior class, as previously established by the already-mentioned writings of the house of Ogasa-wara. Even the traditional clothing for wearing at the Tea Ceremony altered at this time, and a change towards the Japanese style can be detected. In consequence, all laymen of no special rank or standing now wore a common, standard form of ceremonial dress to attend the celebration. Those in monastic orders would wear a priest's robe with a half-length over-garment, while the nobles would wear skirt-like white breeches with the over-garment. Meanwhile Yoshimasa is said to have attended tea gatherings in ceremonial hunting dress.

We can say in conclusion that it was Nōami who, through his work in laying down firm rules, turned the Tea Ceremony, as opposed to the tea competitions, into a special form of social gathering. At the same time he gave the ceremonial a far deeper inner meaning that could not help but exercise considerable influence on the warrior class, most of whom were practitioners of it. In the process he took the first step on the path that would lead in years to come to what is now known as the Tea Way, *chadō*.

In the sixteenth century the rules for the Tea Ceremony became stricter still. The labours of the great Tea Masters began to bear fruit. There was now a Tea Way which was no longer limited to the mere outward form of the ceremony, but which had the effect of transforming the outward procedure into an expression of inner attitude. Here one needs only to consider the seven rules inscribed in the *Shūun'an-hekisho* compiled by Sen no Rikyū and Nambō Sōkei, into which we shall be looking more closely in due course.

Of particular renown in the annals of Japan is the great Tea Ceremony of Kitano (1587), which was arranged by Hideyoshi in collaboration with Rikyū and Tsuda Sōkyū (d. 1591). Details of the invitation to this tea gathering, which was reportedly attended by some eight hundred guests from all levels of society, are given in the *Sōtan-nikki* of Kamiya Sōtan (1551–1635), as well as in the *Taikōki* and the *Kitano-ōchanoyu no ki*. Notices were posted up throughout the length and breadth of the land, explaining in seven paragraphs the purpose of the tea gathering:

> For ten days, weather permitting, commencing on the first day of the tenth month, a great Tea Ceremony will be held in the grove of Kitano, and there, in accordance with the rules, precious tea utensils of every kind will be brought together and displayed for the benefit of tea-lovers.
>
> All those who love the Tea Ceremony – irrespective of whether they are servant lads, merchants or peasants – are to bring with them a water-kettle, a bucket, a water container and something to drink. No objection will be raised if those who have no tea powder bring powdered barley instead.
>
> Since the chosen site is the grove of Kitano, the Tea Ceremony will be performed on two rush mats. Nevertheless no objection will be raised if those who cannot afford these use mats made of rice-straw or even ordinary straw. There will be a free choice of seating position.

There is no question here of a purely Japanese occasion. Anybody so moved may take part, even Chinese.

In order to be able to display everything, even to those from the far provinces, the length of the occasion has been extended to the tenth day of the tenth month.

In view of the fact that this kind of invitation demonstrates a deep sympathy for the impecunious, let anybody who fails to attend bear in mind that, hereafter, even a ceremony performed with roasted barley-powder will be forbidden him, and that he will likewise not be permitted to attend the Tea Ceremony of anybody who himself fails to appear on this occasion.

Anybody who is particularly poor, however far he has travelled, will be presented with tea by Lord Hideyoshi's own hand.

The importance attached by the ruling circles to tea matters can be gauged from the series of decrees setting up special offices devoted exclusively to the culture and preparation of tea. More explicit details on this custom are furnished by the records of the military class, the so-called *bukan* of the Tokugawa period. From them we learn that, in addition to the practising Tea Masters, there were heads of various groups, among them the tea stewards, tea-garden wardens and gardeners. Tokugawa Ietsuna (1651–1680), the fourth Tokugawa Shōgun, issued specific instructions for the maintenance of the tea-room – stipulations whose non-observance carried severe penalties. These instructions were published in the year 1659. Special precautions were taken for the transportation of tea from the tea-gardens of Uji to Edo, the modern Tokyo and capital city of the Tokugawa Shōguns. Everything was regulated down to the smallest detail. The sealed tea-urn was treated like the state treasury. Whole streets were blocked off, and much else besides. Only under the rule of the eighth Tokugawa Shōgun, Yoshimune (1716–1745), were these strict regulations somewhat eased.

The subsequent development of the towns and of the *bourgeoisie* during the Tokugawa period (1600–1868) brought with it a renewed superficialisation of the Tea Ceremony. In brief, it was turned into a personal status symbol. The most beautiful tea-rooms were built, the most exquisite tea utensils acquired – and yet the spirit of the Tea Ceremony was not to be bought for money. Meanwhile, the transmission of the true Tea Way was carried on only within a very small circle. For the rest of society the Tea Ceremony became an exercise in aesthetic dilettantism, and one that was all the more gratifying for the opportunity it provided to outbid others with one's luxurious tea utensils.

The twentieth century, however, with its new political developments and its financial tensions, was to bring about a return to the Tea Way. Once again it was to become a path of self-recollection, a source from which new strength could be drawn, a place of refuge amid the bustle of the material world.

The Tea Way and its Grand Masters: Shukō, Jōō and Rikyū

The first real architect of the Tea Way was Murata Mokichi Shukō (1423–1502), the founder of the Nara or Shukō school. He was the first to be accorded the honorary title of Grand Master, *sōshō*. Born of bourgeois parents resident in the province of Yamato, he entered monastic orders at an early age, becoming a monk in the Shōmyō temple at Nara. He infuriated the priestly officials by his manner, however, and was expelled from the monastery. After long wanderings through the various provinces of Japan he finally came to Kyōto, the capital city. There, in the Shinjūan of the Daitoku temple, he became a pupil of the Zen Master Ikkyū Sōjun (1394–1481). The practice of Zen brought Shukō into closer contact with tea drinking.

This development is entertainingly described in the biography of him given in the *Chajidan*. There it is recounted that Shukō became a Zen monk at the age of thirty. During his studies and meditation exercises, however, an annoying tiredness had a habit of descending on him. For this reason he sought out a well-known physician of his day and asked him for a medicine to combat this tiredness. The doctor recommended Shukō to drink tea. Shukō got hold of some tea from the tea-gardens of Toganoo and soon discovered that the doctor had given him sound advice, whereupon he obtained all the available books on tea and studied them exhaustively. He also collected all the information he could on the procedures observed at the tea gatherings of his day. Finally, on the basis of his own experience of Zen practice, he drew up his own set of rules.

On the completion of his Zen studies, Shukō was presented by his Master Ikkyū, not with the customary seal, but with a hand-written text by Yüan-wu K'o-ch'in (1063–1135), for his safe keeping. This manuscript, a so-called *bokuseki*, is without doubt the tea world's oldest and most famous document of its kind. These *bokuseki* – literally 'ink-marks' – have an important role to play in Zen and the tea teaching. They consist of hand-written documents by well-known Masters, designed either as 'seal'-documents* or to open the way to enlightenment, *satori*, via the medium of a few written signs – or indeed to reveal to the pupil his new name as a monk or an artist. They are expected to transcend the rules of calligraphy, conveying unambiguously the spirit of the writer. Among the Tea Masters these *bokuseki* were almost more highly prized than the ink paintings of the Sung period.

Shukō had the manuscript mounted in the form of a hanging scroll and used it to decorate the alcove of his cell whenever he drank tea there in the manner laid down by his rules. In the process, the realization flashed upon him that the Buddha's law was also inherent in the Tea Way. And at this point we encounter the unity of Zen teaching and tea teaching – that *chazen-ichimi* which is so important for the whole Tea Way.

In his tea teaching Shukō rejected all ostentation – all pomp and luxury. He regarded these as unseemly and far removed from the true Tea Way. He was also fearful that it would lead to the banning of the Tea Ceremony if the merchants of the flourishing trading cities such as Sakai – which was gaining an important position as a port, as a centre for the weaving of gold and silver brocade, and as capital of the province of Izumi – were to take up a form of tea ceremonial which imitated the ostentation of the

* Such a 'seal'-document (*inkajō*) from the Master constituted the pupil's 'graduation certificate'.

warriors and their social circle. Alongside Zen thinking, the influence of other flourishing arts of the time had a role to play in the final formulation of Shukō's Tea Way – notably the art of the Nō play and that of the linked-poem, *renga*. Certainly in his own time his teaching evoked a great response, and the number of its adherents was considerable. It is Shukō whom we have to thank for the fact that the Tea Way ceased to be confined to the warriors and their social circle, and could henceforth extend to simple folk as well.

The contemporary spiritual background was the best imaginable for the development of a Tea Way of the type proposed and realized by Shukō. As a Tea Master he himself had all the necessary qualifications. He was acquainted with the tea customs of Nara, the southern capital, which was the centre of the cultural life of his home province. Yet he was also familiar with the dazzling and splendid tea gatherings of the courtly capital, Kyōto, which stressed outer display to the total exclusion of the spiritual – and indeed were often used as a cover for all kinds of licentious revels. At the same time, the lifestyle of the warriors of the capital city was starting to excite the indignation of the populace. Public posters appeared here and there condemning not only the various depravities to which the upper classes had turned, but also the tea gatherings themselves.

Shukō, totally imbued with Zen, recognized in these developments dangers that could well spell disaster for the people, but he also saw that such dangers could be averted. The Tea Way, it seemed to him, was an ideal means of educating people as individuals and of restoring his contemporaries' self-awareness. And so he duly formulated it on the basis of his experiences in Zen and in conjunction with his other studies and conclusions. Studies in Confucianism, the teachings of the Nō Masters and the poetical writings of eminent poets also gave him much important inspiration for the form and content of his new doctrine.

A particularly revealing light is thrown on Shukō's basic ideas by a letter to his pupil Furuichi Harima (1459–1508), lord of the castle of Furuichi in the province of Yamato, who was closely associated with his followers in the Kōfuku temple at Nara and later himself became a monk.

The worst thing one can do in pursuing this Way is to bear arrogance and self-will in one's heart. It is likewise unseemly to be jealous of one who is proficient or to look down on a beginner. One should closely follow he who is proficient and hearken to his every word, and do one's best to help a beginner to attain maturity. It is important for this Way to wipe out all distinctions between what is Japanese and what is Chinese – this should be borne in mind above all. Moreover, it is quite unpardonable to refer, as at present, to 'cool shrunkenness', where beginners are using tea utensils from the kilns of Bizen and Shigaraki, prizing them even though they are unrecognized by others. 'Shrunkenness' means possessing good tea utensils, correctly understanding their special peculiarities and valuing them out of a true, inner reverence. Then they may justly remain delightful in their 'cool shrunkenness' for all time. For this reason, it is not permissible to deride another's tea utensils merely because his taste does not entirely correspond to one's own. Nevertheless it is well to model one's taste on that of a true connoisseur – that is an important point to bear in mind. Arrogance and self-will are the only true evils here. If, however, the inner (creative) impulse is lacking, then one is following a false Way. The ancients had a word for it: 'Become master of your will; do not let will become your master!'

In these few words Shukō reveals to us the way of

thinking that underlies his Tea Way. The beginner is warned against desire and self-will, exhorted to persevere, impressed with the need for humility; then he will finally discover the true Way. It goes without saying, then, that he will entrust himself to an initiate, to one who has attained maturity on the Way, to a Master.

Shukō lays great stress on the obscuring of the distinctions between Japanese and Chinese. In the tea gatherings of earlier times, things Chinese had held the centre of the stage to an extraordinary extent. From now on, Japanese products from the kilns of Bizen and Shigaraki also gradually started to become fashionable. The question therefore arose quite naturally as to whether these could likewise be used in the Tea Ceremony. Shukō argued for their use, even if the vessels of Japanese origin seemed to lack the elegant taste of Chinese products. It was only towards the end of the sixteenth century, and during the seventeenth, that Japanese pottery would reach its zenith through the efforts of the Tea Masters themselves.

What was the basic difference between Chinese and Japanese tea utensils? The latter at one time lacked the refinement of the Chinese ware. They displayed a peculiar and particularly delightful roughness, brought about by the small pebbles that studded the clay out of which the utensils were made. Moreover many of these vessels even came on to the market with totally unglazed surfaces. Yet it is precisely these peculiarities that give such a special 'feel' to the handler of these utensils. It was their very roughness that enchanted, in contradistinction to the refinement of the Chinese ware. Here, then, Shukō gradually became the pioneer of a re-education of taste, though one that was none too easy to carry out.

At all events, what now gained entry into the tea-room, from Shukō onwards, had the nature of a fascinating paradox. Other Japanese arts, too, had already discovered the road which leads by way of magnificent beauty to simple beauty – to a beauty which does not impose itself on the beholder, and yet which attracts the eye and above all captivates the heart. And so it was that a new ideal cast its spell over the followers of the Tea Way: non-loudness, solemn beauty, perfect imperfection, 'cool shrunkenness'.

But the artist can attain such an ideal only after long practice. It grows only out of personal experience and is a sign of a personal maturity that is no longer influenced by self-will, that is no longer subject to any desires. The artist must free himself from the 'outer', that is to say mere form, and seek the 'inner', the ultimate profundity which alone gives form its meaning. But he can attain this only if his heart is itself no longer attached to outward things, *mushin*. Once he has finally attained that ideal, once a sudden enlightenment allows him to grasp what true beauty is, then he no longer sees, even in 'cool shrunkenness', the process of wilting or withering as a decline in strength, but experiences in it a kind of maturity actually representing the most beautiful of blooms. Now that the world and its fleeting show no longer mean anything to him, and a tranquil, yet living, solitude embraces him, he experiences a beauty that has about it something of the patina of old and venerable objects. And at this point two further concepts, *sabi* and *wabi*, come into play, both being applied to the Tea Way in a very special sense.

It is difficult to define these two concepts unambiguously, since in their deepest sense they have to be felt rather than cognized. 'It shows taste to tie up a noble courser in front of a thatched hut' – this saying of Shukō's contains both *sabi* and *wabi*. The picture of a simple, thatched hut, preferably standing by itself amid a winter landscape, conveys to us the concept *wabi*. And a noble stallion tied up to, or in front of, this simple, lonely hut is *sabi*. Not only does this aesthetic ideal embrace a mere simple beauty, but it has to be a beauty containing within itself the *wabi* feeling – a dark, subdued, yet pregnant beauty, the beauty of maturity. *Sabi* is characterized by the absence of obvious beauty, by the beauty of the colourless as opposed to the resplendent, by the beauty of the perishable as against the exuberantly active, by the beauty of a declining, yet wise, old age as against the beauty of an energetic yet immature youthfulness. The concept *sabi*, then, carries not only the meaning 'aged' – in the sense of 'ripe with experience and insight' as well as 'infused with the patina which lends old things their beauty' – but also that of tranquillity, aloneness, deep solitude.

Consequently, when those 'who do not even possess (particularly good) utensils, but have achieved perfection as regards the three stages of willingness of heart, creative skill and adduced results' are designated *wabi* Masters or *wabi* devotees, this fact is indicative of a new attitude to life. Taking this together with a pronouncement of the *Yamanoe no Sōji ki*, we can begin to appreciate the ultimate goal of the ideal in question: 'If a person has become a Grand Master of the Tea Ceremony and still possesses only one kind of tea utensil, this, to a *wabi* devotee, amounts to total perfection.' Here, then, once again, the right attitude is seen as proceeding from the heart.

Meanwhile, taking the expression, 'still . . . only one kind of tea utensil', we can here detect the first appearance of the 'imperfect' in the Tea Ceremony. And the concept of the imperfect or incomplete is likewise central to the Tea Way as a whole. But there is even more to the concept *wabi* than this. It involves the recognition of the limits of human will in the face of the universe, the respecting of one's fellow-man as one sentient being among an infinite number of sentient beings, together with self-moderation and the will to self-effacement.

On one occasion Shukō, writing to his pupil Furuichi Harima about which rules of conduct were absolutely essential, cited the following:

One's conduct should be natural and inconspicuous.

The flowers should go easily and pleasingly with the room.

In no way should the burning of the incense be performed too rigidly.

The tea utensils should reflect the age or youth of the guests.

The arrangement of the tea-room should be such as to soothe the hearts of hosts and guests, and should in no way distract their thoughts. This is of prime importance. It must penetrate to the very depths of the heart, while having nothing about it of the outer.

> *Why must it be here*
> *that you would spread your fragrance,*
> *you maiden-flower,*
> *where vulgar gossip spreads*
> *its poison in this world?*
>
> SHUKŌ

These words express the spirit of the Tea Way, but at the same time they make clear what is a universally valid, basic rule for Tea People – 'natural and inconspicuous'. Nothing out of the ordinary should disturb the tranquillity of the tea-room or the hearts of the guests. Bound up with this idea is that mysterious bond that exists between man and man. The host opens up his personality to full view – it is conspicuous by its very inconspicuousness. By virtue of the fact that his heart is no longer chained to outward things, he can display his creativity in the highest degree – to such an extent, indeed, that it also draws the guests into its activity. Admittedly his creativity finds its expression in the world of forms, but it far transcends the purely formal, until it touches – if it is true to its nature – the hearts of the guests. But then it is also by way of outward forms that the guest approaches the

47

host. Host and guest – if they are following the same Way – find their way to each other.

From this point on, then, the tea gatherings no longer speak the language of a particular social class, but that of 'everyman', whether he be high or low, rich or poor. All that is needed is that he should open his heart to the Way. A temple of common experience, *ichiza-kenritsu*, is erected, where those of like beliefs, pupils of a *single* Way in quest of an inner harmony that is far removed from the world, find each other on that Way.

Here the basis is laid for the *kei-wa-sei-jaku*, which was later to become to a quite considerable extent the guiding principle of the Tea Way. Only the union of reverence, harmony, purity and tranquillity can bring the Tea Way to its ultimate unfoldment.

Shukō and the bamboo grass

In order to demonstrate by means of a clear example that gorgeous flowers were not the only things that should be on display in the alcove, as worldly taste might seem to indicate, Shukō used to take simple bamboo grass and place it in a vase in the alcove of his tea-room.

Sōchō and his rape-garden

Sōchō loved a weed-grown garden. He completely devastated his well-laid out garden and sowed rape-seed all over it, later thinning out the young plants. Moreover, when meditating in his little hut, he would hang his constant travelling companion – his straw hat – in the alcove in place of a picture-scroll. A truly touching sight.

The One-Sign-Teacher of the plum blossom

In ancient China, under a certain dynasty, there once lived a poet. One day he wrote:

Hard by the forest in the middle of the deep snow
a few plum tree branches last night opened their blossoms.

Then he had a friend listen to this poem. For the friend the expression 'a few plum tree branches' was too weak, and so he altered it to 'one plum tree branch'. This earned him the name 'One-Sign Teacher'.

The Masters were very fond of using these and similar stories to expound their teachings, since they often revealed by concrete example far more than the wordy texts. Indeed, in connection with this last story, which is handed on in almost every school, Shukō declared that it was the guiding principle of his Way, and that anyone who failed to understand what it meant would have great difficulty in gaining entry to the Tea Way.

Shukō had given a new shape and colour to life in the tea world. From the roomy apartments of the *shoin* buildings he had transferred the Tea Ceremony to the little hut with its four-and-a-half mats – the narrow space of the tea-room. To the 'ostentatiously-loud' utensils of Chinese origin he opposed the 'cool and simple'. In place of the black-lacquered *daisu* stood a clean, white, wooden one with simple bamboo supports. Where Chinese tea utensils were formerly employed he made a point of using pieces of a style that expressed *wabi* – and thus also *sabi* – even if they were of inferior materials and quality. He declined to use teaspoons worked in silver or ivory and instead used bamboo ones. Even the flowers were arranged in a simple and pleasing way. His efforts thus helped to produce a Tea Way that was able gradually to free itself more and more from fashions determined by Chinese tastes and to discover a Japanese form of its own. In this way it was at last released from its close association with the warrior classes, and became accessible in its entirety to the common people.

The second Grand Master of the Tea Way was Takeno Jōō (1502–1555). His family came from the province of Wakasa. During the civil wars and disturbances of the Onin period (1467–1477) his grandfather had fallen in battle. Subsequently his father had settled permanently in the city of Sakai and soon made his fortune as a leather wholesaler. It was into this family and its circumstances that Jōō was born. As a result he grew up in a very different environment from Shukō. His father had him brought up in the old, family tradition. In Kyōto he studied the art of poetry under Sanjō Nishi Sanetaka. In the process he heard his teacher expound *Eigataigai*, the work on poetics by Fujiwara Teika (1162–1242), which was to inspire much of the formulation of his own Tea Way. At the instigation of his teacher, the honorific title 'Governor of Inaba, of the fifth courtly rank down' was bestowed upon him in the ninth month of the year 1530. Meanwhile Jōō was also studying linked-verse. But the Tea Ceremony soon came to rank as his chief interest. He studied it under Fujita Sōri, Jūshiya Sōgo and Sōchin – all of them pupils of Shukō – but soon filled it with ideas of his own.

The teaching of Jōō was consequently to give the Tea Way a new face. At the age of thirty-one he took the tonsure and settled first in Sakai, then later in the capital, Kyōto. There he built himself a tea-room. This tea-room's peculiarity was an alcove fitted with a large, round window. The size of the tea-room amounted to a mere three-and-a-half mats. He restricted his tea utensils to sixty selected pieces, all of them displaying both *sabi* and *wabi* – for he enjoyed extraordinary fame as a connoisseur – and these came to be known as 'the exquisite pieces of Jōō'.

Every tea utensil that is too 'loud' (he taught) must be rejected. In the tea-room everything must be in harmony with everything else, utensils with utensils, utensils with flowers, utensils with people. The participants in the ceremony must all do their utmost to ensure that a 'reverent solitude' can arise spontaneously. Yet this can happen only if everything proceeds from a heart that has freed itself from worldly things. By dint of tireless practice one eventually attains the true Way and then becomes, as a tea-person, a 'mirror of humanity'. And at this point a strong emphasis is clearly placed on the Tea Way's practical application.

Jōō frequently uses the expression *shiorashiku kirei*. Within *shiorashiku* we find the word *shioru,* which has the sense of 'wilting, becoming shrivelled, hanging limp', and we need to consider it in relation to what we have already recounted of Shukō. The expression *shiorashiku kirei* denotes a gentle, unobtrusive beauty, such as that of 'the morning-damp blooms of the hedgerow' of which one poem sings to us. Here, too, the insights of the secret Nō tradition are of relevance, as are those of poetics. It is the gentle, unobtrusive, yet echoing beauty that is conveyed to us by the numerous poems of the *Shinkokinshū* (1205), a beauty behind which stands a 'true purity of heart'.

Jōō always knew just how to manifest in his practical work both the beauty required by this ideal and the atmosphere that goes with it. One cold and snowy winter's day, we are told, he placed in the alcove of his tea-room, not the customary flowers, but a container full of clear water. His idea was to underline the pure beauty of the snow, whose very nature is transitory.

'The word *wabi* was used by the poets of former times in many of their poems, but today it means exercising honest and strict self-control and living in humility.' This statement occurs in a communication to his pupil Rikyū, as recorded in the *Kokinchasetsu shū.* 'Keeping oneself under strict control', *tsutsushimi-fukaku,* however, simultaneously carries as a secondary meaning a particular kind of relationship to one's fellow-men – the 'respectful mutual approach'. 'The conduct of the host should convey to the guest a true respect that proceeds from the heart,' and 'even at an ordinary Tea Ceremony, once the guest has followed the garden path to its very end, he should approach the host with the same respect as if this were to be their one and only encounter.' Such are the rules laid down in the *Yamanoe no Sōji ki*.

These thoughts are an allusion to the saying concerning 'the flowers that are an appreciation of the season', for even people cannot overstay their 'season', and nobody knows when his own will come to an end. 'A Tea Ceremony that fails to reach the heart of the guest is unpardonable;' argues Jōō on another occasion, 'it does not reflect the true Way'.

Among the heirs to Shukō's tradition, two Masters stand pre-eminent, Insetsu and Jōō. The later Tea Master Katagiri Sekishu offers the following guide to their basic spiritual attitudes.

The underlying ideas of the three Masters are demonstrated by the following poems:

> *Wherever I look*
> *cherry blossom, crimson leaves,*
> *nowhere to be seen;*
> *a rush-thatched hut by the cove*
> *in the twilight of autumn.*

SHUKŌ

This poem has a profound emotional content. It is one that emphasizes above all the 'solitude and tranquillity' style, *sabitaru tai*. Rikyū was very fond of it.

> *This loneliness!*
> *Not even their colours*
> *do they reveal,*
> *those cedars of the cedar-mountain*
> *in the twilight of autumn.*

INSETSU

This poem displays in its purest form the style known as 'colourlessness', *mushokutai*. (Furuta) Oribe was fond of it; Insetsu founded it.

> *The rain-shower's dew*
> *has not yet vanished.*
> *From the cedars' needles*
> *the mist climbs, fine as a veil,*
> *in the twilight of autumn.*
>
> JŌŌ

This poem is an example of the 'purified serenity' style, *sawayaka naru tai*. (Sen) Dōan loved it; Jōō founded it. In it lies the essence of the Tea Ceremony.

RIKYŪ

Sen Sōeki Rikyū, whose real name was Tanaka, came from Sakai, where his father was a fish merchant. His grandfather, Tanaka Dōetsu Sen'ami, was one of the favourites of the Shōgun Yoshimasa. Rikyū took his name from the written sign *sen* and thereafter called both himself and his house *Sen*. Through his father, Rikyū came into contact with the Tea Way at an early age, and underwent his initial studies with a Master of the Higashiyama school. This was Kitamuki Dōchin, who went on to recommend his unusually talented pupil to Jōō. Consequently Rikyū became familiar with both schools – the capital city tradition of the Higashiyama school and that of the stricter Shukō or Nara school as represented by Jōō. His Zen teacher was the priest Shōrei Shūkin of the Daitoku temple, whence he acquired his Zen name, Sōeki.

Rikyū held Grand Master Shukō in the highest esteem and acquired numerous tea utensils that had once been his. After completing his studies, he settled down in Sakai and worked closely with the two Masters Imai Sōkyū and Tsuda Sōkyū. It was along with these two that he was also summoned to the court of Nobunaga. Later he served in the same capacity under Nobunaga's successor, Toyotomi Hideyoshi, who heaped many honours upon him. Under Hideyoshi he co-operated with Sōkyū on the great Kitano tea gathering. Within the Emperor's household, too, Rikyū enjoyed great prestige, but he declined the offer of courtly rank, and accepted from Tennō only the honorary title of *Koji*. This occurred in the year 1585.

On the twenty-eighth day of the second month of the year 1591, Rikyū ended his life by *seppuku* or knightly suicide, which Hideyoshi had imposed on him.

Rikyū was the great perfector of all the ideas that his two eminent predecessors had set out in their teachings. The available sources show him to have been a man whose heart possessed a deeply-felt compassion, and who appreciated the beauty of the ephemeral just as much as he did that tranquillity which is devoid of inner agitation. He bore in his heart a yearning for *wabi*, and yet was no mere, impoverished monk, living far from the world in his hermitage. Rikyū lived in the very midst of the most turbulent events – indeed it can be said without any fear of contradiction that he played an important part in them. His income was considerable, for he received from Hideyoshi a salary of three thousand *koku* of rice. And yet he remained a true tea-person.

Hideyoshi and the morning-glory

It had come to the ears of Hideyoshi that Rikyū grew wonderful morning-glories in his garden, and that everybody was saying how splendid they were. Consequently he too wanted to see this show of flowers, and informed Rikyū of his intention to pay him a visit. He duly arrived and went into Rikyū's garden. But not a single morning-glory was to be seen. Only when he entered the tea-room did he discover in the alcove a single morning-glory of the most exquisite beauty. Early that morning Rikyū had torn up all the morning-glories in his garden and preserved only this one flower.

The bowl with the plum blossom

One day Hideyoshi summoned Master Rikyū to appear before him. In front of him there stood a golden bowl full of water. Next to it lay a solitary sprig of red plum blossom. 'Arrange this!' commanded Hideyoshi. Rikyū knelt down and, without so much as a moment's hesitation, grasped the sprig with one hand and stripped off all the blossom with the other, so that the petals fell on the water's surface. The petals and buds offered an indescribably beautiful spectacle as they floated on the water. Even Hideyoshi cried out in admiration, 'There was I, hoping to see my Rikyū's troubled face – but it stayed quite untroubled!'

These two tea stories show us Rikyū the real tea-person. He is fully aware of the various tricks that Hideyoshi is liable to play on him, yet he also knows the laws of his Way. And in his wisdom he outmanoeuvres Hideyoshi in a way that is beyond the latter's level of development. Above all, his solution to the problem of arranging the plum blossom in a shallow bowl – a task which by all the rules of flower arrangement is impossible without technical aids – demonstrates the great and skilful creativity of one such as Rikyū, a skill which manages to satisfy at one and the same time the demands of the Tea Way that *sabi* and *wabi* should be observed, and also his own personal rejection of the 'lukewarm'. That is how a tea-person must act, for 'on the Tea Way there is no intellectual cleverness, no half-hearted action: what is alone essential is an inner devotion to the creation of natural beauty. The honourable Jōō said as much. To bring into being something gentle and unobtrusive in the midst of such an unwordly ceremony, rather like an old, gnarled tree bent under the weight of snow, is a difficult thing. What it needs is practice.'

Rikyū sweeps the tea-garden

Rikyū was once given by his teacher, Jōō, the job of sweeping the tea-garden. In fact, however, the garden had already been swept so clean that not a single fallen leaf was to be seen. Rikyū, given the job of re-sweeping a garden that was already so well-swept, went straight out into the garden and, going up to a tree, grasped it with both hands and shook it gently. He watched as four or five leaves gently fluttered down to the ground, and then went back into the house. Master Jōō looked at the garden and commended Rikyū with the words, 'That's what you call real sweeping!'

Rikyū and Jōchi

One snowy winter's evening Rikyū put on his straw cloak and paid an unexpected visit to his friend Jōchi. While walking up the garden path he removed his cloak and his wide-brimmed hat. And there, suddenly, was Jōchi coming to greet him. At once Rikyū drew out of his left sleeve an incense-burner that he had put there to keep his body a little warmer. Without a word he held it out towards Jōchi. The latter took it with his left hand and simultaneously handed to Rikyū his own incense-burner, which he had likewise drawn with his right hand from his own left sleeve.

Rikyū and the stepping-stone

One day the Master was staying at the home of his eldest son, Dōan. While walking up the garden path, he smilingly remarked in a low voice to a fellow-guest, 'One of those stepping-stones sticks up further out of the ground than the others. It must have escaped Dōan's notice.' But his son Dōan overheard this remark and marvelled at his father's fine sensitivity. In an unnoticed moment he adjusted the stepping-stone, taking great care to leave no sign of what he had done. When the Tea Ceremony was over and Rikyū was walking back down the path, he paused on this same stepping-stone and remarked, 'Hm, now it's all right. Dōan must have heard what I said. That's what I call quick work!' And he was delighted.

Rikyū and the sword-stand

Rikyū was already advanced in years before the war-clouds descended on the five inner provinces. Fear and unrest reigned in the hearts of the people. Only in the district of Sakai were things relatively peaceful, and Rikyū could consequently enjoy the Tea Ceremony day in, day out. But during this time of ferment even Rikyū found it difficult to achieve true peace of mind at his Tea Ceremony, for his guests were often great warriors, who came to the tea-room still wearing their swords. In view of this, Rikyū designed a sword-stand and fastened it to the wall by the entrance to the tea-room. Then he greeted his guests with the following words: 'My guests today are all close to my heart and will pardon me a few discourteous words. Nowadays the world is full of turmoil, and people distrust one another. Now, I have installed a sword-stand by the entrance. If my guests do not object, I would ask them kindly to leave their swords there, and *then* to enjoy the tea.'

Dōroku's hoe

One day Rikyū called on Dōroku in Nara, only to find him busy working in his field. They went home together and entered the house. There, standing in the alcove, Rikyū found the hoe that Dōroku had just been using in his field. It was still wet and dirty. Setting up the tool in such a place showed the special value which its owner attached to it, and Rikyū found such taste admirable.

Gentians and chrysanthemums

Both were flowers that Rikyū was not fond of. When cut, they lasted too long and displayed none of the beauty of the moment, of the limited and transitory nature of life.

The tea of Hariya Sōshun

One day when heavy snow was falling, Rikyū was waiting upon his patron Hideyoshi. The conversation ranged over this and that, and eventually the question arose as to who might have a water-kettle on the boil in his tea-room on a day like this. Rikyū expressed the view that his pupil, Hariya Sōshun, certainly would. So, despite the heavy snow, Hideyoshi decided to pay a call on him with Rikyū. Sōshun, who had never expected to be surprised on such a night by Hideyoshi, was utterly astonished, yet he did not show it. Acting on a sudden inspiration, he offered his guests white rice for a cake. The whiteness of the snow as it gleamed out of the dark night, the gentle singing of the water-kettle and the sight of the fresh, white rice – the whole impression of purity evoked the praise of Hideyoshi, and Rikyū was delighted at his pupil's inventiveness.

These tea stories paint a vivid picture of Rikyū. They express his tea ideals, and indicate how spiritual content meant more to him than simple form, even though he was equally keen to have the latter respected. He was concerned not with pedigree or rank, but with people themselves. In fact it was Rikyū who did away with the special entrance to the tea-room, *kininguchi*, reserved for persons of high rank, and replaced it with a lower doorway, *nijiriguchi*, through which one could pass only by bending low. Numerous of the tea rules still in use in our own day go back to Rikyū, and even those arts that have connections with the Tea Way – flower arrangement, pottery and so on – show the strength of his influence. Every action in the tea-room was lived out in all its implications, with content and form standing in inner harmony with each other, while still taking full account of the practical necessities of life.

The seven tea rules known as *Shūun'an-hekisho*, which Rikyū and his pupil Nambō drew up together and inscribed on the wall of the Shūun cell in the Nanshū temple at Sakai, once again reveal to us the teachings of his school:

When the guests have arrived at the waiting-lodge and all the like-minded participants are assembled there, the host announces himself by sounding a wooden gong.

As far as washing the hands is concerned, what really matters on this Way is the purification of the heart.

The host must approach the guests with every respect and conduct them to the tea-room. If the host is a person without composure and imagination, if the tea and eating utensils are of bad taste, and if the natural layout and planning of the trees and rocks in the tea-garden are unpleasing, then it is as well to go straight back home.

As soon as the boiling water sounds like the wind in the pine trees and the sound of a gong rings out, the guests enter the tea-room for the second time. It is unforgivable to let slip the right moment as regards water and fire.

Neither inside nor outside the tea-room let the conversation turn to worldly things: this is a commandment of old.

At a true gathering neither guest nor host has recourse to fine words or smooth airs.

A gathering may not exceed two double hours in length. If, however, this time is exceeded in the course of discussion of the Buddha's teachings and aesthetic matters, that is not objectionable.

The requirement of *kei-wa-sei-jaku*, into which we shall be looking in the next chapter, also derives from these rules. This requirement was Rikyū's ultimate goal, and numerous tea poems draw emphatic attention to it.

> *Whether they are present*
> *or not, good tea utensils,*
> *how unimportant!*
> *The only true Way*
> *has no need of such things.*

> *The garden path!*
> *Far from the fleeting world*
> *it remains a Way to us.*
> *Why not shake off right here*
> *the dust from our hearts?*

> *The Tea Way's essence:*
> *To boil water,*
> *to whisk tea and*
> *to drink it – no more!*
> *This is well worth knowing.*

Garden path, tea-room!
The guest and with him his host
together at tea:
their action is harmony
and nothing stands between them.

Numerous pupils were to carry on the tradition of Master Rikyū. But we shall make special reference here only to one Master who occupies a particularly influential place among Rikyū's successors. This was the lord of the castle of Totomi, Kobori Masakazu, or Enshū (1579–1647), the founder of the Tea Way's Enshū school. He was one of his age's outstanding personalities. Not only does Japan have him personally to thank for the most beautiful garden layouts and buildings, but it also has his influence to thank for the stimulation of almost every area of artistic life. He was not merely a Tea Master, an architect and a landscape gardener; he was also a painter, a poet and a potter in equal measure. He had studied Zen in Kyōto at the Daitoku temple, and it was in its spirit, combined with influences drawn from the teachings of Confucianism, that he lived and worked.

The Tea Way also equipped him inwardly to deal with everyday life. 'Outside the Tea Way there is no Way. Let a person do his utmost for his lord and his parents in loyalty and piety. Let him not neglect household affairs. And above all let no one fail to value his relationships with old friends. In spring the fine veils of mist, in summer the cuckoo calling from its hiding-place among the green leaves, in autumn the dark sky emphasizing the solitude, and in winter the dazzling brightness of the snow – all of these breathe forth the essence of the Tea Ceremony ...' Thus he writes in his *Kobori Enshū kakisutebumi*. And in another place he states, 'Whoever is wedded in his heart to the Tea Way, for him there is no distinction between familiar and unfamiliar, between rich and poor;' and, 'Whoever is striving earnestly on this Way, let him avoid all conceit, or else he will make no progress.'

So it was that the Tea Way continued to be cultivated through the centuries, while minor changes could do little to alter the inner core with which Rikyū had endowed it. Its function, in the words of the Master himself, was to raise man, both in outer form and inner inclination, to truthfulness itself, and thus to take on the function, for anyone experiencing it, of a 'tea ceremonial of liberation'.

The Tea Way and Zen

The Tea Way has been followed by statesmen, commanders-in-chief, warriors, businessmen and monks, some of whom have even become Masters of it. But irrespective of the social class of the followers of this Way, we find hardly one of them who did not pass through the school of a Zen Master in one or other of the great temples or monasteries.

The link between tea and Zen is thus easy to understand, the more so when we consider that it was primarily the priests and monks who brought it to Japan, very often specifically in connection with the practice of their religion. It is thus only to be expected that the ceremonial form of tea drinking should have been strongly influenced by the teaching with which it was so strongly associated. Nothing was more natural than that the Tea Way, once it had become a Way in the Japanese sense of the word, should have striven after the same ideals that characterized its doctrinal 'country of origin'.

The Tea Way, too, is a Way designed to bring man to the annihilation of the ego, to pave the way for the ultimate experience of enlightenment. And the well-known saying on the unity of Tea Way and Zen doctrine, *chazen-ichimi*, thus has every justification. We are informed specifically about this close association in a posthumous work by Sen Sōtan, which was handed down under the title *Chazen-dōitsumi*, but later appeared under another title. A pupil of the Tea Master Takuan of Edo had transcribed it, and in the year 1818 it appeared as *Zencharoku*.

The Zen Way as the heart of tea drinking

The idea of making the Zen Way the heart of tea drinking originated with the Zen Master Ikkyū of the

Purple Heather. For it so happened that Shukō of the Shōmyō temple in the southern capital of Nara became his spiritual pupil. He showed a special *penchant* for everything to do with tea and practised day after day. The Zen Master Ikkyū, observing this, came to the conclusion that the Tea Way accorded excellently with the essential points of the Buddha's teaching. Thus arose the Tea Way, which mirrors Zen ideas in the whisking of the tea, and causes us to reflect in our hearts on behalf of all living beings about the teaching of the Buddha. Thus there is no single aspect of the practice of the tea doctrine which deviates at all from the Way of Zen . . .

If, consequently, a person discovers within himself a serious inclination to Zen-tea, then given a willingness to practise, he has already fulfilled the main prerequisite of our Way. Whisking tea is Zen practice in the truest sense, and a spiritual exercise leading to the clear understanding of our own deeper nature. When it comes to the essence of the doctrine, as Sākyamuni taught it for forty years, the heart is the sole valid means of bringing about the breakthrough of absolute enlightenment on behalf of all worlds and sentient beings. Apart from this there is no other possibility. Sākyamuni presented his teaching in various ways, using moralizing sermons, parables and speeches as his teaching aids. The tea doctrine likewise recognises as valid the use of teaching aids, in its case in the form of the procedure for preparing tea. It is this that now becomes the method of contemplation and the means of revealing the depths of the self . . .

Anyone who scorns the spiritual exercise of Zen-tea, designed as it is to lead to knowledge of the law of life, is like a blind man who destroys himself in despair, or like a person who beats himself with his own fists or belabours his own head. The followers of our school must fulfil this one, great, ethical duty with total reverence, as they practise that true tea drinking which has about it the taste of Zen.

The practice of the tea-doctrine

The essence of the Tea Way lies, not in selecting tea utensils according to their value, nor in discussing their form while the tea is being prepared, but only in entering the state of contemplation in which one spontaneously handles the utensils correctly, and in attaining the religious attitude of heart through which we may grasp the Buddha-nature within us. Now in this respect the religious practice of devoting oneself to the Tea Way as a means of seeking the basis of one's own being is without compare. Possessing a heart that is not shackled to outer things, and handling the tea utensils in this light, is the purpose of one's contemplation. Even if it is only a matter of the handling of the tea-scoop, let a person give his heart unreservedly to this tea-scoop and think of nothing else whatever; that is the correct way of going about it from beginning to end. Even when one lays the tea-scoop aside, let it be done with the same deep devotion of heart as before. And not only does this apply to the tea-scoop – it is similarly valid for the handling of every utensil.

On the true meaning of the tea-doctrine

The true meaning of the tea doctrine is equally the true meaning of Zen doctrine. Anyone who sets aside the true meaning of Zen doctrine will find no meaning in the tea doctrine. One who has no taste for Zen likewise has no taste for tea. On the other hand, the meaning of the tea doctrine as conceived of in profane circles is the mere cultivation of a kind of aestheticism. This cultivated aestheticism is held to be the true meaning of the tea doctrine. People adopt a look of what they imagine to be sublime enlightenment, personal arrogance ensues, others are accorded a totally un-merited contempt, and everyone speaks as though the Tea Masters of this world understood nothing of the true meaning of tea. Alternatively it is asserted that one may not reduce the true meaning of tea to words, nor hand on as a doctrine its outer form: instead, it is said, one should merely know oneself and become en-lightened – a doctrine which is believed to be a form of 'transmission outside the teachings', when in fact all that results is a false theory of enlightenment.

It is hardly possible to stress more strongly the link with the teachings of Zen. As for the interpretation of the four concepts *kei-wa-sei-jaku* – which refer respectively to reverence, harmony, purity and tranquillity, and thereby outline the whole nature of the Tea Way – we are assisted here in a striking manner by a text written by the Tea and Sword Master, Takuan Shūhō, the *Takuan Oshō chatei no ki,* which no doubt arose out of his tea conversations with Kobori Enshū.

Tea-room notes by the honourable Takuan

Chanoyu takes its origin from the spirit of harmonious union between heaven and earth, and thus becomes a vehicle of peace, a means of preserving order in the world. People today, though, turn it more into an opportunity to invite friends, to hold discussions, to enjoy food and drink – in short, into a servant for mouth and stomach. Moreover, they spend all their energy in the tea-room on ostentatious finery, seek out rare and costly utensils, are inordinately proud of their own elegant methods of preparation and laugh at the awkwardness of others. But that is not the original sense of *chanoyu*.

Hence, let a person erect a small hut in the shadow of a bamboo grove or among trees, lay out watercourses and rocks, plant grasses and trees, lay in charcoal, hang a kettle over it, arrange flowers and prepare the tea utensils. For by transplanting all this – rivers and mountains, the nature of streams and rocks – into this single space, it is possible for us to enjoy the seasonal landscapes, the snow, the moon and the flowers, to experience the times when the grasses and trees bloom and decay, and to allow reverence to reign as we greet our guests. We can listen to the water in the kettle, singing like the wind in the pines, forget the cares and worries of the earthly world, and as we allow the waves of the river of *Wei* to flow out of the water-dipper, we wash away all the dust from our heart. Here, truly, is the abode of the holy hermit among men.

'The origin of propriety lies in reverence, and its true application lies in the appreciation of harmony.' So runs a saying of K'ung-tzu, which explains the application of propriety and is at the same time the guideline of the heart in the *chanoyu*. To give an example: when a virtuous man comes together with men of rank, his behaviour towards them should be seemly and simple, yet without servility. And when one is sitting with people of lower estate, let one avoid all disparagement and not be stinting of reverence. Thus there is something present in the 'emptiness' that works through harmony and does not pass away: it endures and moreover commands respect. It is the smile of Kāsyapa, the affirmative nod of Tseng-tzu; it is the meaning of the hidden nature of suchness.

Hence, from the planning of the tea-room right down to the choice of tea utensils, the seemliness of the tea preparation, the seating arrangement, clothing and so on, let nothing disturbing be present, let no desire for ostentatious beauty hold sway. Let a person restore the heart with old tea utensils; let him not forget the landscapes of the four seasons; let him show no servility, no desire, no conceit; let him not neglect to show respect. Simple, honourable, upright behaviour – that is what *chanoyu* is all about. Thus, let a person take a delight in the natural harmony of heaven and earth; let him transplant mountains, rivers, trees and rocks to his own fireside and experience the five elements (within his own self). Let him draw from the source of heaven and earth and savour in his mouth the taste of the wind. Is it not mighty? Pleasure in the spirit of the harmony of heaven and earth – that is the Way of *chanoyu*.

Here, too, then, the practical experience of cosmic wholeness, which lies at the basis of the Buddhist Mahayana teaching, is very much to the fore.

The following legend is recounted of Mahā-Kāsyapa. Once the Buddha was sitting in silence amid his pupils. In his hand he held a flower. The pupils were all gazing at the Master, full of expectancy. Only Kāsyapa was smiling, full of understanding. Then the Master said to him, 'Mine is the full possession of truth, the intangible spirit of Nirvāna, which I bestow on you.' Nobody can attain to ultimate knowledge unless he is determined to overcome rational thinking. It is to this legend that Takuan is alluding here.

Elsewhere in his notes Takuan turns his attention to the concepts of reverence, harmony, purity and tranquillity. These four concepts have an important role to play in the Tea Way. Under Rikyū they are even more strongly emphasized. They too have their origin in Zen. They were the underlying principles of the strict discipline of the Zen monasteries, as the old monastic rules make quite clear. It is also recorded that a pupil of Po-yün Shou-tuan (1045–1072), a Zen Master of the Sung period, elevated these four concepts into the basic verities of communal tea drinking among the monks. Again, as the *Zenrin-chakai-sange-mon* puts it, 'The earthly world is without harmony in its actions, and everybody is ruled by greed, wrath and ignorance. But we live in harmony and reverence, and our every action is pure and tranquil.'

The concept 'reverence', *kei*, comprises deference, respect for other people and at the same time self-control in so far as the ego is concerned: it also includes reverence for all living things. 'Harmony', *wa*, is one's harmonious relationship to all things. This harmony reveals itself in one's personal behaviour, in one's relationships with one's whole environment and in one's self-adjustment to it. It is a concept well-rendered by the expression 'grace of heart'. The combined effect of both concepts is to engender that deep feeling that links man to all other living things and allows him to participate at a really deep level in their own being. One's heart, once it has surrendered itself to these concepts in the Zen sense, no longer has any room for any particular object or circumstance, but devotes itself solely to what is in front of it – in the sense of *mushin* – and thus becomes totally 'gentle and tender', *nagoyaka*. The short poems of Matsuo Bashō reflect this attitude in all kinds of images. For example:

> *Even the wild boar*
> *is pierced through and through*
> *by the storm on the heath.*

> *Winter drizzle!*
> *Even the little monkey*
> *longs now for a cloak.*

Sei, 'purity', is an outer and inner cleanliness which must also be understood in the moral-ethical-religious sense of the term. It is cleanliness rooted in the naturally plain and simple. It is as apparent in the tea utensils, for example, as in the people connected with them. It is a readiness for the ultimate experience, to which the heart must surrender itself in all purity – free of all emotions. The actions of the Tea Way start with the washing of the hands and the rinsing out of the mouth. This takes place during the guest's traversal of the garden path, which leads to the tea-room and conveys him out of the fleeting world of dust towards his purification in the pure world of tea. For 'the Tea Ceremony in its humble, narrow room is a Way which can be trodden only through the religious exercise of the heart, and one in which the Buddha's teaching must stand pre-eminent. To turn the planning of the room and the exquisiteness of the food into a form of entertainment is a mere manifestation of worldliness. To leave the hut imperfect and the food insufficient truly suffices. The Buddha's teaching is the chief content of the Tea Ceremony.' Thus declares Rikyū, and elsewhere he adds that the Tea Ceremony is 'a Buddha-sphere of purity'.

The concept 'tranquillity', *jaku*, is the last and at the same time the most difficult to grasp. It is also the concept that has been subjected to the greatest number of deviations during the Tea Way's history. This tranquillity covers a whole range of ideas. It is a special tranquillity, a tranquillity bound up with peace of heart, with soli-tude – a tranquillity which one experiences and yet which simultaneously resides within one. Yet the concept also covers an ideal of beauty which itself has close associations with the concepts *sabi* and *wabi*. It demands the avoidance of everything loud and obtrusive, of anything which affronts the eye. The keynote of this concept is once again determined by the Way of Zen. For there the concept stands in close association with *satori*, enlightenment.

Worldly desires are extinguished, to be replaced by self-absorption into the 'nothingness'. Thus our concept also embraces that of 'emptiness', *ku*, which is simultaneously that of silence. And at this point we are brought back to the concept of purity. For between this and the concept of silence there is once again a close link in terms of the Tea Way. Alongside the 'pure and unsullied' one also speaks of 'pure and unsullied knowledge'; but then this is none other than 'ultimate wisdom', *chi'e*, or knowing and understanding through the power of intuition – transcendental wisdom. And it is here that the link with the concept 'tranquillity' is to be found, for it is through tranquillity that one experiences the All-Oneness that is the Buddha-nature in the Buddha-sphere.

Let us now return to the *Zencharoku* of Sen Sōtan and hear what else this work has to say to us.

'WABI'

The sign *wabi* is used in the Tea Way with especial reverence, and indicates observance of the Buddha's commandments. However, the people of this world use the term *wabi* to refer to outer phenomena, where inwardly there is no sign of any *wabi* content. What, then, can one say of a person who spends quantities of shining gold on his tea-room to give an outward impression of *wabi*, who exchanges fields and gardens for gorgeous and costly porcelain and then shows off in front of his guests? Can anybody call that a fine taste for *wabi*? True *wabi* is incomplete, shows no self-will and no desire for perfection . . .

The author goes on to give a few examples from literature, and then continues:

Once one has considered the sign *wabi* and its Japanese connotation, the idea can no longer arise that

71

dependence signifies dependence nor, similarly, that imperfection is simply imperfection. Indeed, it should be clearly understood that *wabi* is that incompleteness which in fact contains no thought of incompleteness. If a person interprets dependence as dependence, complains that incompleteness is incomplete and judges the imperfect to be imperfect, then that is not *wabi*, and such a person may justly be described as a poor fool . . .

Provided, then, that one does not get lost in all these intellectual speculations, one will succeed in keeping firmly and unerringly to the spirit of *wabi* – and that amounts to observing the Buddha's commandments. That is why, once a person knows of *wabi*, no greed arises, no flouting of prohibitions, no unruliness, no negligence, no waywardness and no foolishness. From now on, greed is transformed into charity, the flouting of prohibitions into their strict observance, unruliness into forbearance, negligence into serious endeavour, waywardness into inner contemplation and foolishness into wisdom. These are what are called the six *haramitsu* – by which is meant the ability to carry through and complete one's self-transformation into a Bodhisattva. *Haramitsu* is a Sanskrit word, and means in translation 'reaching yonder shore,' *pāramitā*. This signifies treading the path of enlightenment. And since the sign *wabi* is equivalent to the practical application of these six *haramitsu*, should it not then be a commandment of the Tea Way, to be truly held in all honour?

Meanwhile, the words of the *Nambōroku* show us the practical application of this teaching to the Tea Way:

The basic meaning of *wabi* reveals a Buddha-world of spotless purity; therefore let the dust also be immaculately swept from the garden path and the little grass hut. And provided that landlord and guests are of upright heart in their dealings with one another, then the laws of the ceremony, its prescriptions and criteria are of no account whatsoever. The whole thing is but a single procedure, from the making up of the fire, through the boiling of the water to the pouring of the tea. Nothing else is permissible. It is through this that the dew-clear purity of a Buddha-heart finds its expression. If one is too intent on all the ceremonial courtesies, then one merely relapses into all kinds of worldly obligations, so that in the end either the guest is attending to the landlord's careless acts and making excuses for them, or the landlord is amusing himself at the carelessness of the guest. In any case, no period has ever produced a person who grasped the whole thing in all its ultimate refinement and profundity. If Chao Chou were the host and the first Zen patriarch the guest, and if Master Rikyū and I were to sweep the dust from the garden path, that might just about be a perfect gathering.

Here we can see the other, hidden side of *wabi*, and one which reveals to us a totally Buddha face. For *wabi* is also the moral perfection of the Buddha devotee, as applied to the disciple of the Tea Way. It is that which one bears *in* one's heart, yet does not put on outward display all the while it is not in full accord *with* the heart. *Wabi* is 'the joy of a little monk in his wind-torn robe'. It is a conscious poverty which, through knowing about it, is no longer poverty. *Wabi* is the self-sufficiency that the Zen monks and poets used to experience when they set off on their long wanderings in search of ultimate experience. In poverty they roamed the countryside, crossed high mountains, forded wide rivers, traversed lonely, dark forests, and in the process became acquainted with that sense of solitude that responds intimately to every mood of nature. It was here that the wanderers' senses were awakened to the ultimate interrelatedness of things, here that they experienced tranquillity and the great 'emptiness'.

Similar thoughts are expressed by the great Zen Master Ikkyū, who had the strongest influence on the Masters of the Tea Way, for the simple reason that many of them studied Zen under him. Various of his sayings are recorded for us in the *Gaikotsu*, among which we find:

Discard the supposition that there is a self. Simply act in the fleeting ball of vapours that is your body.

All things inevitably become empty, and this emptying process signifies a return to the source of original being. The ideas that may arise in us through this or that association when we are sitting in front of a wall are without reality, and even over fifty years' worth of sermons are devoid of it.

Identical thoughts, expressed in different imagery, are expressed by the poet-monk Matsua Bashō, when speaking of his Way in his travelling diary *U-tatsu-kikō*:

In my body there lives a certain 'something'. Let us tentatively give it a name and call it 'a little monk in his wind-torn robe'. But do we *really* mean the tearing of a thin robe in the wind? For a long time this fellow loved to compose short poems. In fact, he finally made it his life's task. Sometimes, however, he regrets it and would like to give it up: sometimes he is overcome with enthusiasm and experiences the ambition to do better than others at it. Now this, now that, the emotions are at war in his heart, and as a result he is left restless. For a while he was keen to get a job for himself in the outside world, but this 'something' restrained him from doing so. At another time he nurtured the wish to take up the study of the Zen teachings and to enlighten his ignorance, but here, too, the 'something' caused him to give up the idea. And so he has remained unskilled and incompetent, apart from the fact that he has remained constantly bound to a Way. It is the self-same Way sought by Saigyō in his poems, by Sōgi in his linked-verse, by Sesshū in his ink-paintings and by Rikyū in his Tea Ceremony – the one, single Way that is operative in all their works. And whoever loves this Way follows the laws of nature and becomes the friend of the seasons. Whatever he sees turns out to be flowers. Whatever he feels turns out to be the moon. When there are no flowers in what he does, he is like a barbarian. When there are no flowers in what he feels, he is like a wild beast. Forsake the barbaric, cast aside the brutish, follow nature's laws, return to her again.

And in another place:

A longing for the winds and the wandering clouds gripped my heart and I yearned to experience the essence of the flowers and birds.

Here we have the same longing for ultimate knowledge as is revealed in the works of the Tea Masters. Here, too, lies the source of Rikyū's ideas when he calls his form of Tea Way a 'Tea Ceremony of Liberation'. The *Zencharoku* takes up these thoughts and speaks in one of its chapters of transformation through the agency of the tea doctrine. This in turn is reminiscent of what Kitayama Junyu has to say in his *Metaphysics of Buddhism*:

Absolute, true Being (the absolute Nirvana-world) overcomes the evil of knowledge (of polarity). Great love and absolute reason complement each other. Consequently the liberated one remains neither in life nor in death, neither in becoming nor in passing away, neither in being nor in Nirvana. He is active throughout the eternal future in bringing blessings to all

75

sentient beings, and at the same time he lives in the realm of eternal tranquillity.

The quest of the Tea Way, then, is nothing less than the quest for this transformation – in the course of which one must allow nature to have its way, and which may not be consciously sought.

We follow these laws, and when we enter the tea-room we entrust ourselves to the spontaneous workings of nature, renounce our tiny knowledge and draw near to the absolute emptiness and silence: that is what we have to realize from beginning to end. Then again, the distinguishing marks of Zen-tea are but few, and there is no warrant for practising it as something secret or hidden. If, meanwhile, one is drawn to the various tea practices that have been mentioned, and wastes one's time hoping for Buddhahood, then one is not realizing the true Way – and when, in any case, would one then attain the mystery of transformation? But if one preserves the true form of Zen-tea and strives after it in religious devotion and practice, then one will enter automatically into the mystery of transformation.

Through such avenues of thought the Tea Way is eventually extended far beyond the ideals of one such as Rikyū, while the various assorted kinds of Tea Ceremony – be they endowed with the most delightful names such as 'Tea in the Snow', 'Tea with Flowers', 'Tea by Moonlight', 'Tea by the Wood-fire' and the like – are rejected as useless. Practice, the religious exercise of the heart, is the sole essential. Through it one eventually attains enlightenment quite spontaneously, just when one is not expecting it. Moreover, 'one should also know of the sense in which *mu*, the sign for "nothing", affects the lives of guest and host at a true Tea Ceremony. Thus we read in the *Dentōroku* the words: "In the fireplace there is neither guest nor host." '

> *Featureless was the Tea Way in the beginning,*
> *zeal, self-control its only natural law.*
> *Yet, whether there be rules or no,*
> *let one but give up one's will*
> *and, like a miracle, transformation will follow.*

The Tea-Room and Tea-Garden

Tea-room and tea-garden are a harmonius unity, and for this reason will be dealt with together here. The tea-room is quite distinct from any other structure or style in Japanese architecture. If the mighty temple buildings display weight and gravity – emphasized by heavy slate roofs, deeply overhanging eaves and, not least, massive pillars – and so remain as it were memorials for posterity, the character of the tea-room is of an ephemeral nature. The very choice of construction materials demonstrates this. But then it was never intended to be anything more than a 'hermitage' amid this transitory world, granting its occupants a temporary place of refuge. It was with the subsequent development of the tea doctrine that the form and character of the tea-room were eventually to change.

We have already seen how closely tea and its use in Japan were tied up with the life of the monks in the Zen monasteries. Not one of the Tea Masters exercised his craft without first establishing its basis through the study and practice of Zen. What, then, could be more natural than that the spirit and atmosphere of these places of learning should have been reflected in the tea-room? If the temples of other Buddhist sects were primarily centres of prayer and pilgrimage, the Zen temples and monasteries differed from them in this respect too. For they were no more than the monks' living and study accommodation. The temple was where they lived, practised and worked. They sought the meaning of their being within the self, undistracted by the external world.

Zen temples, consequently, are sanctuaries of a special kind. Their rooms are simple and plain, and even the main hall is almost without decoration, revealing none of the customary over-ornamentation of other Buddhist sanctuaries. Only an image of the Buddha, or his pupil Kāsyapa, or of the Zen patriarch Bodhidharma is to be found there. One thinks inevitably at this point of the story of the conversation between Bodhidharma and the Chinese Emperor Wu. Asked by the Emperor what was the meaning of the holy doctrine, the Zen Master replied, 'Where everything is infinite "void", nothing can be called "holy".' Or again, of the story of the priest Tanka who, one icy winter's day, used a wooden statue of the Buddha to light a fire to warm himself. When a monk sought to draw his attention to the sacrilegiousness of his act, Tanka gave his admonisher to understand that he was looking for the precious jewel that is alleged to form in the body of a Buddha after it is burnt. When the monk replied that he would surely find nothing of the kind, Tanka coolly replied that in that case the statue could have been no Buddha, nor his act sacrilegious. Whereupon he returned to warming himself at the fire. And this same spirit of Zen – simple, plain, but profound – was to inform the design of the tea-room.

The Japanese have a variety of terms for the tea-room, each indicative of its form and character. We find such expressions for the tea-room as *chatei, kakoi, sukiya, chaseki, chashitsu, chaya* and *sōan,* to name but a few. The term *chatei* refers to the tea pavilion, as used at the time of the tea competitions. *Kakoi* – the word means 'that which is enclosed' – refers to the Tea Ceremony as held in the apartments of the *shoin* buildings. In this case an area measuring some four-and-a-half mats (*tatami*) would be divided off by screens from the rest of the room, whose total area often measured as much as eighteen mats. In other words, we already have here the standard dimensions of the later tea-room. *Chashitsu* likewise denotes a true tea-room built either onto or completely into a dwelling-house, while *chaseki* is a detached tea-room. *Chaya* and *sōan* refer to a temporary tea-room. The most widely-used expression during the period of the Tea Ceremony's development, however, was *sukiya*, on which we shall have more to say below.

The surviving data reveal that the size of the tea-room was always determined by the number of floor-mats (*tatami*) in use. Since one *tatami* measures roughly ninety centimetres by one hundred and eighty, a four-and-a-half mat tea-room will measure about three metres square. This is the normal size, but alongside it a number of variants also developed. Thus, we find six-mat tea-rooms as well as three, two and one-and-a-half mat versions. Rikyū in particular was fond of decidedly small rooms.

Meanwhile, let us return briefly once more to the term *sukiya*. As we have already seen from the statements of the *Yamanoe no Sōji ki*, fine distinctions were often made among the devotees of the Tea Ceremony, who in those days were commonly referred to as *sukisha*. In particular, those who were well-versed in the utensils and formalities – i.e., who had merely achieved a certain mastery of their craft – were distinguished from those who, in addition, possessed *wabi*. The former were called *sukisha* or even *chanoyu-mono*, while the latter were designated *wabi* Masters, *wabi-sukisha*. The term *suki* signifies 'having a predilection and surrendering oneself totally to it'. It replaced the former expression *monogonomi*, which originally had more or less the same sense; but in the course of time this word acquired a special nuance of its own, being applied more and more to the dilettantes. *Suki* was not originally confined to the Tea Way. The devotees of other arts were likewise referred to as *sukisha*. In later times, however, the term became associated more or less exclusively with tea. Indeed, the Tea Way itself came to be called *sukidō* and its disciples *sukisha* or *sukibito*, while the tea-room acquired the name *sukiya*.

With the development of the Tea Way, the meaning of the term *suki* naturally also underwent change. No longer was it simply a matter of merely surrendering oneself to a personal predilection. The predilection grew into a real enthusiasm for tea utensils of rare beauty, and out of this a collecting mania developed. This, of course, no longer had anything to do with the true Tea Way attitude. As we have seen from the utterances of the various Masters, a true devotee of the tea doctrine firmly rejects anything of the kind. Numerous criticisms of the tendency are voiced in a variety of texts, which we shall forbear to go into here. The true *suki* attitude embraces not so much an enthusiasm for, as a true love of such things, in that they embody, according to their several natures, what is also the inner desire of the true tea-person – reverence, harmony, purity and tranquillity. But, in the process, there is no justification for replacing reverence with rarity value, harmony with symmetry, purity with mere cleanliness, or tranquillity with artificial rigidity. 'If a person uses the word *suki* to mean "a lover of what is fashionable", and displays an affection for outward things, then this deviates quite decidedly from the basic ideas of the Tea Way.' So says the *Zencharoku*, emphasizing on another occasion, 'If one is neither attached to worldly existence, nor a seeker of earthly things, but experiences joy in non-pursuit of the perfect and in personal poverty – such a person in his lonely little hut is called "one who has *suki*" . . . Because, therefore, it involves the inclination to leave things in their imperfect totality, *suki* is like the *wabi* referred to above, rejoicing as it does in pure poverty, offering an end to greedy pleasures and standing very close to the monastic rule.'

These words seem to define the conceptual limits of the *sukiya*. It is not, and should not be, any more than the humble hermitage, the little grass hut, *sōan*, of a person who possesses a refined artistic sensibility in the sense of *wabi* and *sabi*, and who bases his existence on that oneness with nature from which alone ultimate knowledge can spring. And if we also find the tea-room described as 'Hut of Creativity', 'Hut of Incompleteness', 'Hut of Emptiness' and so on, all of these designations are based on the same idea.

'Hermitage in the Mountain Village', 'Hidden Mountain Hut', 'Cell in the Capital City' – these former names for tea-rooms likewise stress the character that is pre-eminent as far as the tea-room is concerned – that of a hermitage. A feeling of remoteness from the bustle of the world – a tranquil, contemplative solitude – is exuded by the whole structure. And this is further emphasized by the siting of the tea-room in the seclusion of the tea-garden. Something of the special atmosphere of such a hermitage is conveyed to us by the *Tōgen'iji*. Described in it is the lonely cell which the Prince of Mito, Tokugawa Mitsukini (1628–1700) erected for himself towards the end of his life, in order to be able to devote himself wholly to his interests amid the peace and tranquillity of nature. He called his little hut 'Hermitage on the West Mountain'.

The Hermitage on the West Mountain is an unusual place. The front roof is thatched with rushes, but, on top of these, *Shibakiri*-grass grows profusely. Ivy climbs up the fence by the gate, and only at the front is there a short stretch of bamboo fencing. On the other sides the hermitage abuts directly on the mountain: here there is nothing that could be called a fence. The rushing water of a spring can be heard clearly as it gushes out at the foot of a rocky plateau. Such a sound might well purify the ears of any inhabitant of this earthly world . . .

The tea-room has about it a spirit both of perfect simplicity and of purity. It is the personal expression of the creative spirit of its Master, and reveals to the guests his innermost being. It reflects Zen ideas on the transitoriness of life and its whole design proclaims its role as a mere, temporary place of refuge during this earthly life, just as the body itself is no more than a temporary shell. The materials of which the tea-room is constructed have a natural simplicity about them. Bamboo, wood, mud, reeds and straw are used – all of them perishable and of natural origin. Irregularity reigns, thus adding a magical imperfection redolent of nature itself. The walls are of mud, and mostly painted in restful colours. Their lower portions are often papered with old letters, pieces of calligraphy and woodprints from books. The tea-room's whole design speaks of incompleteness – in other words, 'perfect imperfection'. This fact, too, bespeaks the spirit of Zen, as we shall see even more clearly when we come to consider the role of painting in the tea-room.

Meanwhile, the architecture of the tea-room bears witness to the important distinction between the new, Zen-influenced attitude of mind and the old, traditional Japanese approach, which deferred to the laws of symmetry and – as many buildings still demonstrate to us – held them in great esteem. On the other hand, the Zen teachings and, by the same token, the Tea Way, attach great importance to assymetry, for only this is free of repetition and so promotes creative development. Besides, the feeling of completeness is too prominent in a symmetrical context, and this is just what is not required. Every repetition also simultaneously gives the impression of a completion, or at very least of a limitation. It is here, in fact, that we may seek the reason for the use of a whole variety of timbers in the tea-room. The post of the alcove is made of a different kind of wood from the pillars of the room or the frames of the sliding doors and windows, which are covered with white rice-paper. Two entrances lead into the tea-room – one for the host and another, lower one for the guests, *nijiriguchi*. In contrast to the Japanese style of building, with its big, sliding windows, the tea-room has only small windows that hardly allow any view of the exterior. Only in this way can the secluded atmosphere be generated which is needed to create that special world that is so remote from the everyday. Everywhere one looks, then, one finds a striving for perfection, but a perfection that stops just short of completeness. The final completion is left to the sympathetic beholder.

The tea-room is empty when the guests first enter it. The utensils and ornaments are brought in only when they are already present. Moreover, they are removed again at the end of the ceremony in the presence of the guests. Only the 'emptiness' remains. Nothing happens in the course of the Tea Ceremony to bring about any conscious climax; its progress is measured and unaccentuated. The guests, as we have already seen, walk up the garden path and enter the 'emptiness' of the tea-room, and at the end of the ceremony they walk back down the garden path again, leaving the 'emptiness' behind. But this 'emptiness' is, at the same time, that which is All-Enveloping: only through it can the tea-disciple attain ultimate truth.

> *Tree of wisdom, nothing of the kind exists,*
> *Not even a mirror on its stand.*
> *There is nothing whatsoever to be real,*
> *So how should there be anything for dust to settle on?*

The guest is led to the tea-room by the garden path, *roji*, which passes through the tea-garden. This path stands as a kind of symbol for the whole tea doctrine. It was above all Master Rikyū who laid particular emphasis on the design of the *roji*. He even named his whole teaching 'The Tea Way of the grass-grown hut on the dew-covered path', *roji-sōan no chadō*. In this way he revealed the whole basis of his outlook: a great love of the universe in its multifarious but simple beauty, as manifested in the bright, morning dew, a symbol of purity which, as it glistens on the moss of the path and hangs on the thatched roof of the hut, serves as a reminder of the transitoriness of all things.

A hidden spring pours its clear water into a stone basin, or a watercourse crosses the garden, the pebbles on its bottom gleaming up through its crystal-clear waters. A few trees, which in autumn clothe themselves in a robe of brocade, stand by the path or over against the tea-room. Here and there groups of grotesquely-shaped rocks protrude from the shrubbery. Thick green mosses or lichens cover the ground. Only the stepping-stones stand clear, showing the traveller the way through this world of living silence to the tea-room. The groups of rocks, the watercourse, the thick moss – all remind one of the mountain solitude of the old Zen temples. Far from the world! – this is the atmosphere to be cultivated. The landscaping of the tea-garden is ideally designed for showing the guest whether its creator is familiar with the concepts *wabi* and *sabi*. The garden path is the way to the world of tea in more senses than one. For it also engenders inner readiness of heart. From the symbolic point of view, it is the first step on the Way to enlightenment. It is here that self-absorption begins, that the heart is purified, and that the great forgetting takes possession of man. With every step along the garden path the heart loosens its links with the world.

The beauty of the garden must be so devised that one is not consciously aware of it. It must simply be there, fulfilling the heart, without producing any notion of its own existence. The harmony of the whole layout must be such as to cause the heart to resonate in sympathy.

The garden is often enclosed by a wall, whose presence emphasizes even more strongly its isolation from the everyday world. Particularly evocative, as Ikenaga Sōsaku writes, is a simple mud wall, such as often encloses a lonely mountain temple.

Depending on the tea school, one also sometimes finds an outer and an inner *roji*, the two being in this case separated from each other by a gate. On the outer garden path lies the waiting-pavilion, *machiai*, as described in the introduction to this book.

Even the form of garden layout differs according to the tea school in question – but this difference is no more than one of form, the nature of the garden itself being scarcely affected. The same laws are observed in almost every case. The outstanding Master in the art of tea-garden layout is said to have been Kobori Enshū, and many of his creations have remained intact for posterity. Let us listen once more to the *Zencharoku* as it speaks to us of the tea-room and tea-garden:

The garden path

Turning our attention to the tea-gardens of the present day, we find that these vary considerably from each other, and not least in the matter of 'inner' and 'outer' paths. In the original sense of the word 'garden path', *roji, ro* was interpreted as 'to manifest', and *ji* as 'heart'. Thus its meaning was 'to reveal one's inner nature'. 'Garden path' signified eradicating the eternal suffering of the world along with its root causes, and manifesting the Buddha-nature of eternal truth and reality. What is also referred to as 'the white-dewed path', *hakuroji*, is the same thing. 'White', *haku*, means 'totally pure'. It was on the basis of this interpretation that the tea-room was given the name *roji*, in that it is the temple in which the Buddha-nature is manifested within us. Thus, 'garden path' is merely another name for the tea-room ... There is no difference between the two. The tea-room is also called 'another world', and in this it can be seen in its proper relationship to our own heart.

Master Rikyū created in his garden the same atmosphere that is expressed in the already-quoted poem by Shukō:

Wherever I look
cherry blossom, crimson leaves
nowhere to be seen;
a rush-thatched hut by the cove
in the twilight of autumn.

Such is the solitude that the Master seeks. It is a solitude that he and his guests can savour together – or which he can enjoy all by himself. Kobori Enshū seeks the same solitude and tranquillity in a different way:

Pale evening moon!
From afar the sea gleams
between the trees.

This self-discovery via such a mood is experienced by nobody more strongly than the already mentioned *haikai* poet Matsuo Bashō, when he feels himself becoming totally suffused by the heart's enlightenment:

What a stillness!
Deep into the rock sinks
the cicada's shrill.

The Tea Way and Flowers

The art of flower arrangement holds an important position in Japanese life. Just as one speaks of a Tea Way, so also there is a Flower Way, *kadō*. In the Flower Way we find – just as with other Ways – a variety of schools with differing rules and regulations.

The most ancient school of flower arrangement traces its teachings to the time of Crown Prince Shōtoku (572–621), and sees its progenitor in the later lay-priest Ono no Imoko, who lived in the capital, Kyōto, in the neighbourhood of the Rokkakudō of the Chōbō temple. His house bore the name 'Cell by the Fishpond', *Ikenobō*, which was later adopted as the name of the first school. What is known for a fact is that this art developed into a teaching in its own right during the period of the Ashikaga Shōgunate (14th to 15th centuries). The custom of placing flowers in front of the Buddha's picture was already well-known long before this. Various works of Japanese literature, largely stories and diaries, testify to the fact. Flowers, incense and candle-stand all came together in front of the Buddha's picture. Moreover, it is reported in the *Konjaku-monogatari* that people would go into the mountains to pick the season's flowers and offer them, together with the incense, in honour of the Buddha.

We have already noted this custom in connection with the tea competitions. Furthermore, the artistic advisers of the Ashikaga Shōgun Yoshimasa – the Masters Nōami, Sōami and others – likewise enjoyed for the most part a reputation as Flower Masters. The development of the alcove in Japanese house construction subsequently ensured that the flower arrangement retained an honoured place within it. To start with, it still stood in front of a picture of the Buddha or of one of the saints, but later it came to be placed in front of other pictorial adornments, or even to stand by itself. It was at this point that the complex system of rules of the Ikenobō school came into being. People of all classes started to enjoy the art, and soon it was flourishing, duly encouraged even further by the development of the tea teaching. Right up until the arrival of the great Tea Masters, the strict form of flower arrangement represented by the Ikenobō school reigned supreme in the alcove. This kind of flower arranging was called *rikka* or *tatebana*. Strict rules and a strongly emphasized symbolism held sway.

The essential points of any arrangement are the trinity of *shin, soe* and *tai*. The interpretation of these concepts differs somewhat from school to school, but in principle all of them nevertheless share the same underlying meaning. *Shin*, the vertical stem governing the whole arrangement, embodies truth, heaven, the Buddha himself; *tai* represents the body, matter, man; and mediating between the two, *soe*, the Bodhisattva, assists in the attainment of enlightenment. In the esoteric tradition of the Tanigawa school, the *Sendensho*, we are told: '*Shin* should be seen as Buddha, *soe* as a helping deity and the lowest grasses as people.' A bloom strongly indicative of the season is always used as *shin*. A twig can also stand in its place. But under the influence of the tea doctrine rather less emphasis gradually came to be placed on the *shin*. An 'incomplete arrangement' was now called for. Here too, then, there arose a movement away from 'conspicuous' beauty.

Once the Flower Way had achieved familiarity and popularity, even among townspeople, the over-strict rules of the *rikka* schools were no longer rigidly observed. A new version of the art developed – one that was directed towards a more naturalistic goal. It was known by the name *nage'ire*, and quickly established a relationship with the Tea Way, whose ideals it reflected far more than did those of the *rikka* schools. The new movement no longer used heavy vessels, largely of bronze, as its flower holders, but turned instead to flower holders fashioned out of simple bamboo, or made of bamboo wickerwork, and designed to act either as hanging vases or as standing vases. In such containers it was of course impossible to 'arrange' the flowers in the strict *rikka* sense. Now one could only 'drop them in', *nage'ire*, in a virtually random bunch. No longer, then, would human planning, with all its artifice, have any role to play by achieving a formal design, as it had necessarily done under the *rikka* school. That role was now taken over by the flower itself, seen as a living presence. *Nage'ire* follows a method of arrangement designed to reproduce nature on the basis of the flower's own laws of existence. In it, man has only a mediatory role to play. Thus we see almost the same transformation taking place in the art of flowers as in the Tea Way – a change away from the purely formal and towards the simple and natural. In the case of flowers, 'arranging', *tateru*, is replaced by 'putting in', *nage'ireru*. And in the tea-room the latter is finally transformed into merely 'keeping alive', *ikeru*. The present-day expression for flower arranging, *ikebana*, reflects this fact.

At the same time, however, we should not overlook the fact that the Tea Masters had a quite different attitude to flowers. For the Flower Masters the arranging of the flowers was an end in itself. For the Tea Masters, on the other hand, the arrangement was no more than one aspect of the overall procedure of the Tea Ceremony. The flowers – in the context of the tea-room their arrangement is called 'tea-flowers', *chabana* – have a special function to fulfil. They bring the time of year into the tea-room. They must therefore embody the environment in which they live. They must reveal in their arrangement something of their particular nature. The Master who arranges them can no longer concentrate merely on matters of craftsmanship. His whole heart must be in the flower if he would grasp its essential nature. What he endeavours to reveal through his arrangement is not the beauty of the flower, but the flower as a fellow-being in its own right. From this it follows inevitably, however, that the arrangement of the *chabana* can follow no set rules, since the nature of each flower demands a different arrangement. Satisfying this requirement is the main point at issue. At the same time the Master has to take care that the flowers do not clash with the tea utensils, and that everything fits in harmoniously with everything else. Whereas, for the most part, the Flower Master seeks to create a harmony with the immediate environment – the room, the hanging scroll and so on – the Tea Master additionally endeavours to create with the aid of the flowers harmony with a wider environment – with the universe itself.

The Tea Way and Painting

Whenever no flowers are present at the Tea Ceremony, a picture-scroll, *kakemono*, is to be found hanging in the alcove. For the most part the picture is a simple ink-drawing but sometimes this is lightly colour-tinted. In this sphere, too, we may claim that the Tea Way has brought its influence to bear – this time, through the use of paintings in the Tea Ceremony, on the art of painting generally, and on the appreciation of black-and-white painting in particular. And here, too, it goes without saying that the teachings of Zen are at work behind the scenes.

When looking at oriental paintings, we Europeans encounter similar difficulties to those we find when confronted with a flower arrangement. We may well enjoy looking at a Japanese picture, but does this enjoyment really spring from a deep understanding, from inner experience? We observe its forms with delight, and experience a decidedly aesthetic pleasure – but perhaps for the wrong reasons! Are we really able to see the piece of art through the eyes of true understanding? Mere awareness of its form, of its technique, is not enough. In the Far East, 'understanding' is achieved only when we can feel the resonance that a work produces within us, once we have truly grasped its innermost nature. It is important, then, if we are fully to 'appreciate' a picture, that we should experience it in the Japanese sense. This is made easier for us if the picture is in a Japanese room, and all the more so if it is in the alcove.

The Japanese room, after all, is otherwise without adornment. The eye is not distracted by other things. The picture and the flower arrangement in the alcove occupy the centre of our attention. The picture's lines and dots etch out a melody of their own. It comes to life only when that melody starts to sound in the heart of the beholder.

Thus it is that, as in the story by Lieh Tzu, the melody of the lute-player Po Ya resonates within the heart of his friend. It is the self-same experience. It is called 'resonance', *yoin*.

Pride of place in the tea-room is accorded to the ink-painting, the black-and-white picture. Yet even this kind of painting is full of secrets. Such paintings are in the truest sense of the term mirrors of their Masters' souls. Every brush-stroke, every line, every dot, even every white, 'empty' space has its meaning. The conversations of the Zen Masters with their pupils, their attempts to awaken enlightenment in them through non-explanation, are designed as signposts for those who do not yet know. Only the overcoming of all mental preconceptions renders the pupil ready for the miracle of 'enlightenment'.

Ink-paintings, too, are nothing less than a method of handing on acquired experience to the pupil. The representation of an object in the picture is not undertaken because of its shape or form. The Master's one and only object is to transmit an experience – the 'Oneness' that he himself has experienced as an initiate. He absorbs himself totally into this 'Oneness', be it lotus, bamboo or crane. He experiences the object's innermost being and then represents it. But the work becomes complete in the Zen sense only when his pupil has experienced the 'Oneness' that resides within the work. Artistic appreciation is here transformed into meditation. And in this sense Japanese art is 'frameless' – i.e., the picture is not limited by a frame, either in the physical or in the mental sense. It places a high premium on the active participation of the observer.

A Far Eastern Master once declared that a mountain is to be seen in every stone, the sea in every drop of water. In other words, it is always the cosmic whole that needs to be grasped, the experience of that cosmic whole that needs to be realized. When we look at ink-paintings, we find represented in them not this or that landscape, but landscape as such, landscape as a natural experience. Nature is in a state of perpetual change. And so at the same time we are led to recognize the law of existence. Decay and becoming are also basic to human life. Consequently, this feeling also predominates in ink-painting.

Ceaseless is the flowing of the passing river, and yet its water is never the same. The foam that floats on still water, now vanishing, now accumulating, does not last long. So it is, too, with the people of this world and their dwellings.

These words of Kamo no Chōmei (1153–1216), from his *Hōjōki*, and the following passage from the *Tsurezure-gusa* of Yoshida Kenkō (1283–1350), make it evident that this law of existence, this awareness of the perpetual change of nature, is an innate, ever present feeling.

If one were to live for ever and not fade away like the dew on the field of Adashi, or blow away like the smoke over Mount Toribe, how could one sense that melancholy that pervades all things? For it is the very transitoriness of the world that makes it so beautiful.

> *The autumn's approach,*
> *not yet is it apparent*
> *for the eyes to behold;*
> *yet the sharpness of the wind*
> *gives a sudden feeling of it.*
>
> FUJIWARA TOSHIYUKI

The object of the painter's quest is the underlying nature of things, their cosmic relevance, but not their form. So it is that the paintings constantly reflect a personal quest for knowledge: they are self-confessions. Such an evaluation is certainly merited by the true ink-paintings. They are creations after the style of the tea-room, intended simply and solely for the benefit of their creators, or at most for a few initiates. They are totally subjective, and bear witness to their Master's innermost being and his footsteps along the Way.

At which point it becomes obvious that ink-painting was virtually made for the Tea Way. The alternative, objective style of painting, which represents things from a totally human point of view – as the eye sees them – pursues a practical goal in its quest for a measure of originality, but is consequently of no use to the tea-person. And so the essential point in painting, just as in the construction of the tea-room, reduces once again to the notion of 'perfect imperfection'.

As Kakuzō Okakura writes: 'The dynamic nature of this philosophy laid more stress upon the process through which perfection was sought than upon perfection itself.' For this reason we encounter the 'unexpressed' just as often in ink-paintings as in Zen conversations. At exhibitions of ink-paintings I have often heard friends express the view that they are 'only sketches'. We Europeans tend not to appreciate the total and fulfilling expressiveness of these pictures. At the same time we are conscious of a lack of harmony. Yet this, too, is intentional, for in this area also the practitioners are wary of the danger of limitation or repetition that completeness can bring with it.

The white – 'empty' – space in the ink-painting, *yohaku*, is symbolic of 'that which is unexpressed', that 'perfect imperfection'. And within that 'emptiness' is concealed the 'resonance' that plays an equally important role in Japanese poetry. What the brush does not paint, the 'initiate' must feel in his heart. That is where the picture, the poem, or the flower arrangement in the Tea Ceremony finds its completion. Such people as we find depicted in the ink-paintings are figures of hermits, saints, poets, priests – 'initiates' all – who are no longer attached to earthly things. From the minute size of their representations it becomes apparent that they are mere incidentals:

they are never treated as foreground. They embody tranquillity, reflection, introspection. The ways in which they are represented spring from the painter's own spiritual attitude. What is man? He is no more than a minute speck in relation to the whole: he is insignificant. And so here he is reduced to a mere means of conveying that immensity.

Turning to the relative valuations placed upon ink-painting and water-colour painting by advocates of the Tea Way, we find in the *Usoshū* that water-colour painting is appropriate for flowers and fruit, but that ink-painting is suitable only for landscape, bamboos and trees, and distant, misty mountains. It is further stated that the 'imperfect' nature of this black-and-white painting fits in particularly well with the Tea Way, since the heart has to come to the aid of the beholder. 'In the ink-painting a little temple peeps from behind the trees of a village, sandbanks and rapids show amid a river, and that part of the landscape that is not visible can be earnestly sensed in the heart' – here speaks the outlook of the Tea Masters of the time. It reveals an extraordinary admiration for ink-painting, as brought to Japan from the China of the Sung period. Yet this admiration does not derive from the viewpoint of artistic criticism, but is based solely on a subjective appreciation of the picture in question. Pictures by great Masters were not the only ones that were held in high esteem: in fact the artist's name did not come into it at all. The real criterion was what any given picture had to say – whether it was capable of exciting a resonance in the heart of the beholder.

In this connection an amusing story is told of Dōan, Rikyū's son. He once wrote under a picture the title 'Fish in Clear Water'. But the picture showed nothing: there was only the emptiness of the white paper. This could be seen as the ultimate example of the idea of 'completing the incomplete in the heart'.

The already-mentioned *bokuseki* – examples of calligraphy mounted as picture-scrolls – were held in particularly high regard. At this point it is important to bear in mind that in the Far East the words 'write' and 'paint' are represented by the same written sign, and that writing is done with brush and ink. Even the brush technique as such derives from the same basic calligraphic rules.

Alongside the *bokuseki*, the next most admired pictures took the form of portraits of Masters or priests, *chinsō*, though these differed markedly from the objective type of portraiture, *nise'e*. Both *bokuseki* and *chinsō*, meanwhile, were widely used as 'seal'-documents. By presenting him with a seal, *inka*, the Master expressed his final recognition of his pupil and bestowed on him his new name as a Master.

We may conclude, then, by saying that the contemporary Tea Masters took no account either of fashion or of the painter's name. It is noticeable that ink-painting began to decline in Japan only after it had started to slip from the grasp of the Zen priests and the Tea Masters, to be taken up by painters professionally as a means of earning a living. It was from then onwards that names began to become important, with 'glitter' often counting for more than 'gold'.

He who would admire the beauty of the moon
should not direct his gaze at the pointing finger!

The Tea Way and the Tea-Person

The Tea Way is intimately bound up not merely with almost every Japanese art, but also with life itself. It embodies in its outward aspect a special kind of aestheticism. Seen from the inward point of view, it constitutes an attitude to life – indeed, a whole *Weltanschauung*. And it has been influenced not merely by the Zen teachings, but also by Taoism. If I have not referred specifically to Taoism in the course of this study, it is because it came to Japan in close association with Zen. Many of its ideas, indeed, had already found their way into the Zen teachings. Meanwhile it may be that various of the rules governing the handling of the tea utensils owe something to Taoist influence. To an extent it helped to neutralize the sense of polarity inherent in existence. It is difficult to describe, but one senses this immediately a Japanese takes hold of the tea-bowl, for example. The left hand supports it, while the right hand grasps it in such a way that one has the impression that hand and bowl have become one. The hand conforms to the bowl and the bowl to the hand. It is here that the 'doing-nothing', the *wu-wei*, of Taoist doctrine seems to have found its manifestation.

In the influences of the two doctrines we can see the reason why the Tea Way has no doctrinal system of its own. The rules for the sequence and form of the individual actions do not provide a doctrinal framework for the Tea Way's spiritual message. And when one attempts to construct such a system according to the laws of logic, it soon becomes apparent that there is really nothing there. One merely loses sight of the vital point amid a mass of words. There *is* a vital point to the tea teaching, but it can be illustrated only through its practice and its history. It is also demonstrated by the great Tea Masters, eminent tea-people who lived out their teaching in their lives. The

Tea Way is a source from which man (and especially modern man, who finds himself beset by the problems of everyday existence as never before) can draw new strength. Hence, no doubt, the fact that in today's Japan so many busy people – businessmen, politicians, for example – are devoted to the Tea Way. It grants man a sense of liberation, a freedom that is simultaneously a form of security. It translates him into a condition where earthly things are no longer of any significance. It is the strict rules and laws that have to be mastered by the celebrant, the firmly laid-down sequence governing the performance of individual actions, that provide the basis for this sense of freedom. This arises once the practictioner of the Tea Way has become free of them in his heart, in that he himself has *become* the law, and the law himself.

In connection with the ultimate grasping and experiencing of these basic teachings, we also have to bear in mind what the tea doctrine calls the secret transmission, *hiden*, which was handed on by the Master of each school to his spiritual heir – that is to say, to the future transmitter of his teaching tradition. The true 'secret doctrine' has nothing in common with the outer forms by means of which it is transmitted. These are merely teaching aids, in the Buddhist sense, to help the disciple experience the inner meaning that cannot be expressed in words. In ink-painting, for example, the human figure is present in the picture, if at all, only to give, by simple contrast, a feeling of space which cannot actually be represented.

Within the attitudes which underlie the Tea Way, however, original Japanese characteristics are also to be found. The love of purity, of nature, of tranquillity and simplicity – all these are qualities that are native to the Japanese. In the Tea Way they are exaggerated on a philosophical and religious basis, extended upwards and outwards beyond man himself, until he too is drawn willy-nilly along with them. He himself becomes a part of the Tea Way, a product of his own handiwork.

At the present time, we often find the purely aesthetic side of the Tea Way very much overdone. In the process the Way loses much of its authenticity. The core of *kei-wa-sei-jaku* is lost – that mutual willing-heartedness which resides in a total surrender to the Whole, which exudes goodness and benevolence, and to which the aesthetic arrangements merely give external form. The essential point is not form, but the personality of the host and the goodwill that proceeds from his heart towards the guests. The tea-room knows no high and low, but only knower and non-knower. The low entrance-door, *nijiriguchi*, of the tea-room forces every guest to his knees. The room must be entered in humility. And the guests are all equally dear and important to the host. There can be no esteem based on rank or status. To this extent the Tea Way contains within it a truly democratic element. One is forcibly reminded of a story that Fukukita Yasunosuke tells of the elderly Baron Takashi Masuda in his book *Chanoyu*.

Baron Masuda was once invited to a Tea Ceremony by a simple artisan who lived in a suburb of Tokyo. He accepted, and set out on the day appointed. At an early stage in the journey he had to abandon his rickshaw, as the alleyways that led to his host's house were too narrow even for this form of transport. As he passed a public fountain in which a simple man was cleaning a fish, he asked him the way to the house that he was looking for. It transpired that it was this very man who was to be the host. He duly accompanied his guest to his very humble abode. Baron Masuda was the only guest. The room was a two-mat room. While the host was preparing the fish, his guest simply had to wait patiently. But then he found set before him a meal that was admittedly simple, but nevertheless prepared with great love and care. The cutlery was plain and cheap, but of sound taste. After a suitable interval, the guest was invited into a somewhat larger room, where he was offered tea. The tea utensils were equally simple and humble, but arranged with refined sensitivity, and in such harmony with the plain and simple nature of the host! The latter now related with a certain humble pride his equally simple life-story, and so engaged his guest in conversation. And at this point the wealthy nobleman bowed to the simple artisan, and they joined each other over a bowl of tea.

This is an excellent story for demonstrating the power of the Tea Way. The wealthy nobleman, who has in his possession several tea-rooms and can even call some of the tea utensils of Kobori Enshū his own, finds himself in the company of a simple artisan in a side-street of a suburb of Tokyo – a man who does not even own a tea-room and whose tea utensils not only lack the venerability of age, but actually exhibit – dare one say it? – a cheap simplicity. And yet the two of them are no more and no less than two simple men meeting each other on a single Way. They do not merely meet and pass each other by, but experience Oneness, because they are nothing other than their own true, honest selves, free of all constraints.

The Tea Way has a part to play even in the everyday life of modern Japan. It moulds the behaviour and moral attitudes of individuals whatever their place in human society, and thus has an influence on family lifestyles. And that is without considering here the further, aesthetic impulses that are detectable in architecture, in landscape gardening, in everyday implements and even in clothing.

Certainly the Tea Way is not a Way for the many, even if many follow it. Only a few initiates attain its ultimate goal, finding in the Tea Way the path to the true Self. They become free of concern for the transitoriness of all earthly things; they partake of the eternal; they rediscover nature, because they are in harmony with all living beings.

> Blown away by the wind,
> The smoke of Mount Fuji
> Vanishes into the sky!
> Where do they go, who knows,
> The wishes of my dreams?
>
> SAIGYŌ HŌSHI

Bibliography

Baltzer, F., *Das japanische Haus*, Berlin, 1903.

Benl, O., and Hammitzsch, H., *Japanische Geisteswelt*, Baden-Baden, 1956.

Berliner, A., *Der Teekult in Japan*, Leipzig, 1930.

Bohner, H., *Akaji Sōtei – Zen-Worte im Tee-Raum*, Tokyo, 1943.

Fukukita, Y., *Chanoyu*, Tokyo, 1932.

Furuta, Sh., 'Zen no bunka' in *Gendai Zen-kōza*, Vol. 3, Tokyo, 1956.

Gulik, R. H. van, 'The Lore of the Chinese Lute' in *Monumenta Nipponica* II/2, Tokyo, 1939.

Hammitzsch, H., 'Wegbericht aus den Jahren U-tatsu' in *Sino-Japonica*, Festschrift Andrê Wedemeyer, Leipzig, 1956;

'Zum Begriff "Weg" im Rahmen der japanischen Künste' in *Nachrichten der Gesellschaft für Natur- und Völkerkunde Ostasiens*, No. 82, Wiesbaden, 1957;

'Zu den Begriffen *wabi* und *sabi* im Rahmen der japanischen Künste' in *ibid*, Nos. 85–86, Wiesbaden, 1959;

'Das Zencharoku des Jakuan Sōtaku. Eine Quellenschrift zum Tee-Weg' in *Oriens Extremus* 11/I, Wiesbaden, 1964;

see Benl, O.

Iguchi, K., *Chadō-yōgo-jiten*, Kyoto, 1952.

Izuyama, Z., 'Zen to cha' in *Chadō-zenshū*, Vol. I.

Kitayama, J., *Metaphysik des Buddhismus*, Berlin, 1941.

Kuwata, T., *Nihon no chadō*, Tokyo, 1954;

Seami to Rikyū, Tokyo, 1954;

ed., *Chadō-jiten*, Tokyo, 1956;

'Katagiri Sekishū' in *Chadō-Zenshū*, Vol. II.

Morioka, A., 'Riku-u to Chakyō' in *Chadō-zenshū*, Vol. I.

Nishibori, I., *Nihon Chadō-shi*, Osaka, 1940;
  'Shukō-kenkyū' in *Chadō-zenshū*, Vol. 5.
Okabe, K., *Shumi no chadō*, Tokyo, 1930.
Okada, Sh., *Chami*, Tokyo, 1951.
Sen, S., *O'cha no michishirube*, Kyoto, 1957;
  Ura-Senke Chanoyu, Kyoto, 1957.
Suzuki, D. T., *Zen und die Kultur Japans*, Stuttgart, 1941.
Suzukida, K., *Chawa*, Tokyo, 1952.
Tanaka, S., 'Wa-kei-sei-jaku no kai' in *Chadō-zenshū*,
  Vol. I.
Yoshida, T., *Japanische Architektur*, Tübingen, 1952.

SELECTED SOURCES

Chadō-zenshū, Sogensha, Tokyo, 1935–6.
Gunsho-ruijū, Keizai-zasshiza, Tokyo, 1897–1902.
Zoku Gunsho-ruijū, Keizai-zasshiza, Tokyo, 1923–30.
Nihon-kotenbungaku-taikei, Iwanami-shoten, Tokyo,
  1957–68.